J. H. DOU(

INDIAN CLUBS

AND

DUMB BELLS

Elibron Classics
www.elibron.com

**Binding is in Blue Cloth with
Cover Design Stamped in Gold**

PRICE **$2.00** NET

Size, 5⅜ x 8 inches;
600 Pages
115 Full Page Plates
Including a Series of
Cartoons by
Homer C Davenport

America's National Game
By A. G. SPALDING

PRICE, $2.00 NET

A book of 600 pages, profusely illustrated with over 100 full page engravings, and having sixteen forceful cartoons by Homer C. Davenport, the famous American artist.

No man in America is better equipped to write on all the varied phases of the National Game than is A. G. Spalding. His observation and experience began when the game was young. He gained fame as a pitcher forty years ago, winning a record as player that has never yet been equalled. He was associated with the management of the pastime through trying years of struggle against prevailing evils. He opposed the gamblers; he fought to eradicate drunkenness; he urged and introduced new and higher ideals for the sport; he was quick to see that ball playing and the business management of clubs, at the same time and by the same men, were impracticable; he knew that ball players might be quite competent as magnates, but not while playing the game; he was in the forefront of the fight against syndicating Base Ball and making of a Nation's pastime a sordid Trust; he was the pioneer to lead competing American Base Ball teams to a foreign land; he took two champion teams to Great Britain in 1874, and two others on a tour of the world in 1888-9; he was present at the birth of the National League, and has done as much as any living American to uphold and prolong the life of this great pioneer Base Ball organization.

When A. G. Spalding talks about America's National Game he speaks by authority of that he does know, because

EAST AND WEST, NORTH AND SOUTH
"PLAY BALL"

he has been in the councils of the management whenever there have been times of strenuous endeavor to purge it from abuses and keep it clean for the people of America —young and old

In this work Mr. Spalding, after explaining the causes that led him into the undertaking, begins with the inception of the sport; shows how it developed, by natural stages from a boy with a ball to eighteen men, ball, bats and bases; gives credit for the first scientific application of system to the playing of the game to Abner Doubleday, of Cooperstown, N. Y.; treats of the first Base Ball club; shows how rowdyism terrorized the sport in its early days; how gambling and drunkenness brought the pastime into disfavor with the masses, and how early organizations were unable to control the evils that insidiously crept in. He then draws a series of very forceful pictures of the struggle to eradicate gambling, drunkenness and kindred evils, and shows how the efforts of strong men accomplished the salvation of the great American game and placed it in the position it occupies to-day—the most popular outdoor pastime in the world.

Interspersed throughout this interesting book are reminiscences of Mr. Spalding's own personal observations and experiences in the game as player, manager and magnate, covering a period of many years. Some of these stories deal with events of great import to Base Ball, and others have to do with personal acts and characteristics of players prominent in the game in earlier days—old time favorites like Harry and George Wright, A. C. Anson, Mike Kelly, Billy Sunday and others.

This book should be in the library of every father in the land, for it shows how his boy may be built up physically and morally through a high-class pastime. It should be in the hands of every lad in America, for it demonstrates the possibilities to American youth of rising to heights of eminent material success through a determined adherence to things that make for the upbuilding of character in organizations as well as of men.

Mailed postpaid on receipt of price by any Spalding store (see list on inside front cover), or by the publishers,

AMERICAN SPORTS PUBLISHING COMPANY
21 Warren Street, New York

Spalding's Athletic Library

A. G. SPALDING

Anticipating the present ten-dency of the American people toward a healthful method of living and enjoyment, Spalding's Athletic Library was established in 1892 for the purpose of encouraging ath-letics in every form, not only by publishing the official rules and records pertaining to the various pastimes, but also by instructing, until to-day Spalding's Athletic Library is unique in its own par-ticular field and has been conceded the greatest educational series on athletic and physical training sub-jects that has ever been compiled.

The publication of a distinct series of books devoted to athletic sports and pastimes and designed to occupy the premier place in America in its class was an early idea of Mr. A. G. Spalding, who was one of the first in America to publish a handbook devoted to athletic sports, Spalding's Official Base Ball Guide being the initial number, which was followed at intervals with other handbooks on the sports prominent in the '70s.

Spalding's Athletic Library has had the advice and counsel of Mr. A. G. Spalding in all of its undertakings, and particularly in all books devoted to the national game. This applies especially to Spalding's Official Base Ball Guide and Spalding's Official Base Ball Record, both of which receive the personal attention of Mr. A. G. Spalding, owing to his early connection with the game as the leading pitcher of the champion Boston and Chicago teams of 1872-76. His interest does not stop, however, with matters pertaining to base ball; there is not a sport that Mr. Spalding does not make it his business to become familiar with, and that the Library will always maintain its premier place, with Mr. Spalding's able counsel at hand, goes without saying.

The entire series since the issue of the first number has been under the direct personal supervision of Mr. James E. Sullivan, President of the American Sports Publishing Company, and the total series of consecutive numbers reach an aggregate of considerably over three hundred, included in which are many "annuals," that really constitute the history of their particular sport in America year by year, back copies of which are even now eagerly sought for, constituting as they do the really first authentic records of events and official rules that have ever been consecutively compiled.

When Spalding's Athletic Library was founded, seventeen years ago, track and field athletics were practically unknown outside the larger colleges and a few athletic clubs in the leading cities, which gave occa-sional meets, when an entry list of 250 competitors was a subject of com-ment; golf was known only by a comparatively few persons; lawn tennis had some vogue and base ball was practically the only established field sport, and that in a professional way; basket ball had just been invented; athletics for the schoolboy—and schoolgirl—were almost unknown, and an advocate of class contests in athletics in the schools could not get a hearing. To-day we find the greatest body of athletes in the world is the Public Schools Athletic League of Greater New York, which has had an entry list at its annual games of over two thousand, and in whose "elementary series" in base ball last year 106 schools competed for the trophy emblematic of the championship.

While Spalding's Athletic Library cannot claim that the rapid growth of athletics in this country is due to it solely, the fact cannot be denied that the books have had a great deal to do with its encouragement, by printing the official rules and instructions for playing the various games at a nominal price, within the reach of everyone, with the sole object that its series might be complete and the one place where a person could look with absolute certainty for the particular book in which he might be interested.

In selecting the editors and writers for the various books, the leading authority in his particular line has been obtained, with the result that no collection of books on athletic subjects can compare with Spalding's Athletic Library for the prominence of the various authors and their ability to present their subjects in a thorough and practical manner.

A short sketch of a few of those who have edited some of the leading numbers of Spalding's Athletic Library is given herewith:

JAMES E. SULLIVAN

President American Sports Publishing Company; entered the publishing house of Frank Leslie in 1878, and has been connected continuously with the publishing business since then and also as athletic editor of various New York papers; was a competing athlete; one of the organizers of the Amateur Athletic Union of the United States; has been actively on its board of governors since its organization until the present time, and President for two successive terms; has attended every championship meeting in America since 1879 and has officiated in some capacity in connection with American amateur championships track and field games for nearly twenty-five years; assistant American director Olympic Games, Paris, 1900; director Pan-American Exposition athletic department, 1901; chief department physical culture Louisiana Purchase Exposition, St. Louis, 1904; secretary American Committee Olympic Games, at Athens, 1906; honorary director of Athletics at Jamestown Exposition, 1907; secretary American Committee Olympic Games, at London, 1908; member of the Pastime A. C., New York; honorary member Missouri A. C., St. Louis; honorary member Olympic A. C., San Francisco; ex-president Pastime A. C., New Jersey A. C., Knickerbocker A. C.; president Metropolitan Association of the A. A. U. for fifteen years; president Outdoor Recreation League; with Dr. Luther H. Gulick organized the Public Schools Athletic League of New York, and is now chairman of its games committee and member executive committee; was a pioneer in playground work and one of the organizers of the Outdoor Recreation League of New York; appointed by President Roosevelt as special commissioner to the Olympic Games at Athens, 1906, and decorated by King George I. of the Hellenes (Greece) for his services in connection with the Olympic Games; appointed special commissioner by President Roosevelt to the Olympic Games at London, 1908; appointed by Mayor McClellan, 1908, as member of the Board of Education of Greater New York.

WALTER CAMP

For quarter of a century Mr. Walter Camp of Yale has occupied a leading position in college athletics. It is immaterial what organization is suggested for college athletics, or for the betterment of conditions, insofar as college athletics is concerned. Mr. Camp has always played an important part in its conferences, and the great interest in and high plane of college sport to-day, are undoubtedly due more to Mr. Camp than to any other individual. Mr. Camp has probably written more on college athletics than any other writer and the leading papers and magazines of America are always anxious to secure his expert opinion on foot ball, track and field athletics, base ball and rowing. Mr. Camp has grown up with Yale athletics and is a part of Yale's remarkable athletic system. While he has been designated as the "Father of Foot Ball," it is a well known fact that during his college career Mr. Camp was regarded as one of the best players that ever represented Yale on the base ball field, so when we hear of Walter Camp as a foot ball expert we must also remember his remarkable knowledge of the game of base ball, of which he is a great admirer. Mr. Camp has edited Spalding's Official Foot Ball Guide since it was first published, and also the Spalding Athletic Library book on How to Play Foot Ball. There is certainly no man in American college life better qualified to write for Spalding's Athletic Library than Mr. Camp.

DR. LUTHER HALSEY GULICK

The leading exponent of physical training in America; one who has worked hard to impress the value of physical training in the schools; when physical training was combined with education at the St. Louis Exposition in 1904 Dr. Gulick played an important part in that congress; he received several awards for his good work and had many honors conferred upon him; he is the author of a great many books on the subject; it was Dr. Gulick, who, acting on the suggestion of James E. Sullivan, organized the Public Schools Athletic League of Greater New York, and was its first Secretary; Dr. Gulick was also for several years Director of Physical Training in the public schools of Greater New York, resigning the position to assume the Presidency of the Playground Association of America. Dr. Gulick is an authority on all subjects pertaining to physical training and the study of the child.

JOHN B. FOSTER

Successor to the late Henry Chadwick ("Father of Base Ball") as editor of Spalding's Official Base Ball Guide; sporting editor of the New York Evening Telegram; has been in the newspaper business for many years and is recognized throughout America as a leading writer on the national game; a staunch supporter of organized base ball, his pen has always been used for the betterment of the game.

TIM MURNANE

Base Ball editor of the Boston Globe and President of the New England League of Base Ball Clubs; one of the best known base ball men of the country; known from coast to coast; is a keen follower of the game and prominent in all its councils; nearly half a century ago was one of America's foremost players; knows the game thoroughly and writes from the point of view both of player and an official.

HARRY PHILIP BURCHELL

Sporting editor of the New York Times; University of Pennsylvania and Columbia University; editor of Spalding's Official Lawn Tennis Annual; is an authority on the game; follows the movements of the players minutely and understands not only tennis but all other subjects that can be classed as athletics; no one is better qualified to edit this book than Mr. Burchell.

GEORGE T. HEPBRON

Former Young Men's Christian Association director; for many years an official of the Athletic League of Young Men's Christian Associations of North America; was connected with Dr. Luther H. Gulick in Young Men's Christian Association work for over twelve years; became identified with basket ball when it was in its infancy and has followed it since, being recognized as the leading exponent of the official rules; succeeded Dr. Gulick as editor of the Official Guide.

JAMES S. MITCHEL

Former champion weight thrower; holder of numerous records, and is the winner of more championships than any other individual in the history of sport; Mr. Mitchel is a close student of athletics and well qualified to write upon any topic connected with athletic sport; has been for years on the staff of the New York Sun.

MICHAEL C. MURPHY

The world's most famous athletic trainer; has been particularly successful in developing what might be termed championship teams; now with the University of Pennsylvania; during his career has trained only at two colleges and one athletic club, Yale and the University of Pennsylvania and Detroit Athletic Club; his most recent triumph was that of training the famous American team of athletes that swept the field at the Olympic Games of 1908 at London.

DR. C. WARD CRAMPTON

Succeeded Dr. Gulick as director of physical training in the schools of Greater New York; as secretary of the Public Schools Athletic League is at the head of the most remarkable organization of its kind in the world; is a practical athlete and gymnast himself, and has been for years connected with the physical training system in the schools of Greater New York, having had charge of the High School of Commerce.

DR. GEORGE J. FISHER

Has been connected with Y. M. C. A. work for many years as physical director at Cincinnati and Brooklyn, where he made such a high reputation as organizer that he was chosen to succeed Dr. Luther Halsey Gulick as Secretary of the Athletic League of Y. M. C. A.'s of North America, when the latter resigned to take charge of the physical training in the Public Schools of Greater New York.

DR. GEORGE ORTON

On athletics, college athletics, particularly track and field, foot ball, soccer foot ball, and training of the youth, it would be hard to find one better qualified than Dr. Orton; has had the necessary athletic experience and the ability to impart that experience intelligently to the youth of the land; for years was the American, British and Canadian champion runner.

HARRY A. FISHER

Graduate Manager of Athletics at Columbia University. Recognized as the leading authority on basket ball in the college world; played on the Columbia 'Varsity team for three years, for two years of which the team did not meet a defeat in the intercollegiate schedule; coach of the team for six years, three of which were championship teams; played on the 'Varsity base ball team of 1903, and was manager of the foot ball team of 1904; member of the New York Athletic Club.

FREDERICK R. TOOMBS

A well known authority on skating, rowing, boxing, racquets, and other athletic sports; was sporting editor of American Press Association, New York; dramatic editor; is a lawyer and has served several terms as a member of Assembly of the Legislature of the State of New York; has written several novels and historical works.

R. L. WELCH

A resident of Chicago; the popularity of indoor base ball is chiefly due to his efforts; a player himself of no mean ability; a first-class organizer; he has followed the game of indoor base ball from its inception.

DR. HENRY S. ANDERSON

Has been connected with Yale University for years and is a recognized authority on gymnastics; is admitted to be one of the leading authorities in America on gymnastic subjects; is the author of many books on physical training.

CHARLES M. DANIELS

Just the man to write an authoritative book on swimming; the fastest swimmer the world has ever known; member New York Athletic Club swimming team and an Olympic champion at Athens in 1906 and London, 1908. In his book on Swimming, Champion Daniels describes just the methods one must use to become an expert swimmer.

GUSTAVE BOJUS

Mr. Bojus is most thoroughly qualified to write intelligently on all subjects pertaining to gymnastics and athletics; in his day one of America's most famous amateur athletes; has competed successfully in gymnastics and many other sports for the New York Turn Verein; for twenty years he has been prominent in teaching gymnastics and athletics; was responsible for the famous gymnastic championship teams of Columbia University; now with the Jersey City high schools.

CHARLES JACOBUS

Admitted to be the "Father of Roque;" one of America's most expert players, winning the Olympic Championship at St. Louis in 1904; an ardent supporter of the game and follows it minutely, and much of the success of roque is due to his untiring efforts; certainly there is no one better qualified to write on this subject than Mr. Jacobus.

DR. E. B. WARMAN

Well known as a physical training expert; was probably one of the first to enter the field and is the author of many books on the subject; lectures extensively each year all over the country.

W. J. CROMIE

Now with the University of Pennsylvania; was formerly a Y. M. C. A. physical director; a keen student of all gymnastic matters; the author of many books on subjects pertaining to physical training.

G. M. MARTIN

By profession a physical director of the Young Men's Christian Association; a close student of all things gymnastic, and games for the classes in the gymnasium or clubs.

PROF. SENAC

A leader in the fencing world; has maintained a fencing school in New York for years and developed a great many champions; understands the science of fencing thoroughly and the benefits to be derived therefrom.

SPALDING ATHLETIC LIBRARY

Giving the Titles of all Spalding Athletic Library Books now
in print, grouped for ready reference

No. SPALDING OFFICIAL ANNUALS

No.	Title
1	Spalding's Official Base Ball Guide
1A	Spalding's Official Base Ball Record
1C	Spalding's Official College Base Ball Annual
2	Spalding's Official Foot Ball Guide
2A	Spalding's Official Soccer Foot Ball Guide
3	Spalding's Official Cricket Guide
4	Spalding's Official Lawn Tennis Annual
5	Spalding's Official Golf Guide
6	Spalding's Official Ice Hockey Guide
7	Spalding's Official Basket Ball Guide
7A	Spalding's Official Women's Basket Ball Guide
8	Spalding's Official Lacrosse Guide
9	Spalding's Official Indoor Base Ball Guide
10	Spalding's Official Roller Polo Guide
12	Spalding's Official Athletic Almanac
12A	Spalding's Official Athletic Rules

Group I. Base Ball

No.1 *Spalding's Official Base Ball Guide*
No. 1A Official Base Ball Record.
No. 1C College Base Ball Annual.
No. 202 How to Play Base Ball.
No. 223 How to Bat.
No. 232 How to Run Bases.
No. 230 How to Pitch.
No. 229 How to Catch.
No. 225 How to Play First Base.
No. 226 How to Play Second Base.
No. 227 How to Play Third Base.
No. 228 How to Play Shortstop.
No. 224 How to Play the Outfield.
No. 231. {
How to Organize a Base Ball League. [Club.
How to Organize a Base Ball
How to Manage a Base Ball Club.
How to Train a Base Ball Team
How to Captain a Base Ball
How to Umpire a Game. [Team
Technical Base Ball Terms.
}
No. 219 Ready Reckoner of Base Ball Percentages.
No. 350 How to Score.

BASE BALL AUXILIARIES
No. 348 Minor League Base Ball Guide
No. 352 Official Book National League of Prof. Base Ball Clubs.
No. 340 Official Handbook National Playground Ball Assn.

Group II. Foot Ball

No.2 *Spalding's Official Foot Ball Guide*
No. 344 A Digest of the Foot Ball Rules
No. 324 How to Play Foot Ball.
No. 2A *Spalding's Official Soccer Foot Ball Guide.*
No. 286 How to Play Soccer.
No. 335 How to Play Rugby.

FOOT BALL AUXILIARIES
No. 351 Official Rugby Foot Ball Guide.
No. 332 Spalding's Official Canadian

Group III. Foot Ball Guide. Cricket

No.3 *Spalding's Official Cricket Guide.*
No. 277 Cricket and How to Play It.

Group IV. Lawn Tennis

No. 4 *Spalding's Official Lawn Tennis Annual.*
No. 157 How to Play Lawn Tennis.
No. 279 Strokes and Science of Lawn Tennis.
No. 354—Official Handbook National Squash Tennis Association.

Group V. Golf

No. 5 *Spalding's Official Golf Guide*
No. 276 How to Play Golf.

Group VI. Hockey

No. 6 *Spalding's Official Ice Hockey Guide.*
No. 304 How to Play Ice Hockey.
No. 154 Field Hockey.
No. 188 {
Lawn Hockey.
Parlor Hockey.
Garden Hockey.
}
No. 180 Ring Hockey.

HOCKEY AUXILIARY
No. 256 Official Handbook Ontario Hockey Association.

Group VII. Basket Ball

No. 7 *Spalding's Official Basket Ball Guide.*
No. 7A *Spalding's Official Women's Basket Ball Guide.*
No. 193 How to Play Basket Ball.

BASKET BALL AUXILIARY
No. 353 Official Collegiate Basket Ball Handbook.

SPALDING ATHLETIC LIBRARY

SPALDING ATHLETIC LIBRARY

Group I.   Base Ball

No. 1—Spalding's Official Base Ball Guide.

 The leading Base Ball annual of the country, and the official authority of the game. Contains the official playing rules, with an explanatory index of the rules compiled by Mr. A. G. Spalding; pictures of all the teams in the National, American and minor leagues; reviews of the season; and a great deal of interesting information. Price 10 cents.

No. 1A — Spalding's Official Base Ball Record.

Contains records of all kinds from the beginning of the National League and official averages of all professional organizations for past season. Illustrated with pictures of leading teams and players. Price 10 cents.

No. 1C—Spalding's Official Collegiate Base Ball Annual.

Contains matters of interest exclusively for the college player; pictures and records of all the leading colleges. Price 10 cents.

No. 202—How to Play Base Ball.

Edited by Tim Murnane. New and revised edition. Illustrated with pictures showing how all the various curves and drops are thrown and portraits of leading players. Price 10 cents.

No. 223—How to Bat.

There is no better way of becoming a proficient batter than by reading this book and practising the directions. Numerous illustrations. Price 10 cents.

No. 232—How to Run the Bases.

This book gives clear and concise directions for excelling as a base runner; tells when to run and when not to do so; how and when to slide; team work on the bases; in fact, every point of the game is thoroughly explained. Illustrated. Price 10 cents.

No. 230—How to Pitch.

A new, up-to-date book. Its contents are the practical teaching of men who have reached the top as pitchers, and who know how to impart a knowledge of their art. All the big leagues' pitchers are shown. Price 10 cents.

No. 229—How to Catch.

Every boy who has hopes of being a clever catcher should read how well-known players cover their position. Pictures of all the noted catchers in the big leagues. Price 10 cents.

No. 225—How to Play First Base.

Illustrated with pictures of all the prominent first basemen. Price 10 cents.

No. 226—How to Play Second Base.

The ideas of the best second basemen have been incorporated in this book for the especial benefit of boys who want to know the fine points of play at this point of the diamond. Price 10 cents.

No. 227—How to Play Third Base.

Third base is, in some respects, the most important of the infield. All the points explained. Price 10 cents.

No. 228—How to Play Shortstop.

Shortstop is one of the hardest positions on the infield to fill, and quick thought and quick action are necessary for a player who expects to make good as a shortstop. Illus. Price 10 cents.

No. 224—How to Play the Outfield.

An invaluable guide for the outfielder. Price 10 cents.

No. 231—How to Coach; How to Captain a Team; How to Manage a Team; How to Umpire; How to Organize a League; Technical Terms of Base Ball.

A useful guide. Price 10 cents.

No. 219—Ready Reckoner of Base Ball Percentages.

To supply a demand for a book which would show the percentage of clubs without recourse to the arduous work of figuring, the publishers had these tables compiled by an expert. Price 10 cents

No. 350—How to Score.

A practical text book for scorers of base ball games, both amateur and expert. The most complete book of instruction on the art of scoring that has yet been published. An appendix includes answers to numerous problems which arise in scoring a game and is of great value in deciding what course to pursue when an intricate point in the rules arises. Compiled by J. M. Cummings. Price 10 cents.

SPALDING ATHLETIC LIBRARY

BASE BALL AUXILIARIES.

No. 348—Minor League Base Ball Guide.

The minors' own guide. Edited by President T. H. Murnane, of the New England League. Price 10 cents.

No. 352—Official Handbook of the National League of Professional Base Ball Clubs.

Contains the Constitution, By-Laws, Official Rules, Averages, and schedule of the National League for the current year, together with list of club officers and reports of the annual meetings of the League. Price 10 cents.

No. 340—Official Handbook National Playground Ball Association.

This game is specially adapted for playgrounds, parks, etc.; is spreading rapidly. The book contains a description of the game, rules and list of officers. Price 10 cents.

Group II. Foot Ball

No. 2—Spalding's Official Foot Ball Guide

Edited by Walter Camp. Contains the new rules, with diagram of field; All-America teams as selected by the leading authorities; reviews of the game from various sections of the country; scores; pictures. Price 10 cents.

No. 344—A Digest of the Foot Ball Rules.

This book is meant for the use of officials, to help them to refresh their memories before a game and to afford them a quick means of ascertaining a point during a game. It also gives a ready means of finding a rule in the Official Rule Book, and is of great help to a player in studying the Rules. Compiled by C. W. Short, Harvard, 1908. Price 10 cents.

No. 324—How to Play Foot Ball.

Edited by Walter Camp, of Yale. Everything that a beginner wants to know and many points that an expert will be glad to learn. Snapshots of leading teams and players in action, with comments by Walter Camp. Price 10 cents.

No. 2A—Spalding's Official Association Soccer Foot Ball Guide.

A complete and up-to-date guide to the "Soccer" game in the United States. Contains instructions for playing the game, official rules, and interesting news from all parts of the country. Illustrated. Price 10 cents.

No. 286—How to Play Soccer.

How each position should be played, written by the best player in England in his respective position, and illustrated with full-page photographs of players in action. Price 10 cents.

No. 335—How to Play Rugby.

Compiled in England by "Old International." Contains directions for playing the various positions, with diagrams and illustrations. Price 10 cents.

FOOT BALL AUXILIARIES.

No. 332—Spalding's Official Canadian Foot Ball Guide.

The official book of the game in Canada. Price 10 cents.

No. 351—Official Rugby Foot Ball Guide.

The official handbook of the Rugby game, containing the official playing rules, referee's decisions, articles on the game in the United States and pictures of leading teams. Price 10 cents.

Group III. Cricket

No. 3—Spalding's Official Cricket Guide.

The most complete year book of the game that has ever been published in America. Reports of special matches, official rules and pictures of all the leading teams. Price 10 cents.

No. 277—Cricket; and How to Play it.

By Prince Ranjitsinhji. The game described concisely and illustrated with full-page pictures posed especially for this book. Price 10 cents

SPALDING ATHLETIC LIBRARY

Group IV. Lawn Tennis

No. 4—Spalding's Official Lawn Tennis Annual.

Contents include reports of all important tournaments; official ranking from 1885 to date; laws of lawn tennis; instructions for handicapping; decisions on doubtful points; management of tournaments; directory of clubs, laying out and keeping a court. Illustrated. Price 10 cents.

No. 157—How to Play Lawn Tennis.

A complete description of lawn tennis; a lesson for beginners and directions telling how to make the most important strokes. Illustrated. Price 10 cents.

No. 279—Strokes and Science of Lawn Tennis.

By P. A. Vaile, a leading authority on the game in Great Britain. Every stroke in the game is accurately illustrated and analyzed by the author. Price 10 cents.

No. 354—Official Handbook of the National Squash Tennis Association.

Contains the constitution, list of members, official playing rules, glossary of technical terms, directions for building a court and scores of national championship and other important matches. Illustrated. Price 10 cents.

Group V. Golf

No. 5—Spalding's Official Golf Guide.

Contains records of all important tournaments, articles on the game in various sections of the country, pictures of prominent players, official playing rules and general items of interest. Price 10 cents.

No. 276—How to Play Golf.

By James Braid and Harry Vardon, the world's two greatest players tell how they play the game, with numerous full-page pictures of them taken on the links. Price 10 cents.

Group VI. Hockey

No. 6—Spalding's Official Ice Hockey Guide.

The official year book of the game. Contains the official rules, pictures of leading teams and players, records, review of the season, reports from different sections of the United States and Canada. Price 10 cents.

No. 304—How to Play Ice Hockey.

Contains a description of the duties of each player. Illustrated. Price 10 cents.

No. 154—Field Hockey.

Prominent in the sports at Vassar, Smith, Wellesley, Bryn Mawr and other leading colleges. Price 10 cents.

No. 188—Lawn Hockey, Parlor Hockey, Garden Hockey.

Containing the rules for each game. Illustrated. Price 10 cents.

No. 180—Ring Hockey.

A new game for the gymnasium. Exciting as basket ball. Price 10 cents.

HOCKEY AUXILIARY.

No. 256—Official Handbook of the Ontario Hockey Association.

Contains the official rules of the Association, constitution, rules of competition, list of officers, and pictures of leading players. Price 10 cents.

Group VII. Basket Ball

No. 7—Spalding's Official Basket Ball Guide.

Edited by George T. Hepbron. Contains the revised official rules, decisions on disputed points, records of prominent teams, reports on the game from various parts of the country. Illustrated. Price 10 cents.

SPALDING ATHLETIC LIBRARY

No. 7A—Spalding's Official Women's _ Basket Ball Guide.

Edited by Miss Senda Berenson, of Smith College. Contains the official playing rules and special articles on the game by prominent authorities. Illustrated. Price 10 cents.

No. 193—How to Play Basket Ball.

By G. N. Messer. The best book of instruction on the game yet published. Illustrated with numerous pictures and diagrams of plays. Price 10 cents.

BASKET BALL AUXILIARY.

No. 353—Collegiate Basket Ball Handbook.

The official publication of the Collegiate Basket Ball Association. Contains the official rules, records, All-America selections, reviews, and pictures. Edited by H. A. Fisher, of Columbia. Price 10 cents.

Group VIII. Lacrosse

No. 8—Spalding's Official Lacrosse Guide.

Contains the constitution, by-laws, playing rules, list of officers and records of the U. S. Inter-Collegiate Lacrosse League. Price 10 cents.

No. 201—How to Play Lacrosse.

Every position is thoroughly explained in a most simple and concise manner, rendering it the best manual of the game ever published. Illustrated with numerous snapshots of important plays. Price 10 cents.

Group IX. Indoor Base Ball

No. 9—Spalding's Official Indoor Base Ball Guide.

America's national game is now vieing with other indoor games as a winter pastime. This b ok contains the playing rules, pictures of leading teams, and interesting articles on the game by leading authorities on the subject. Price 10 cents.

Group X.   Polo

No. 10—Spalding's Official Roller Polo Guide.

Edited by A. W. Keane. A full description of the game; official rules, records; pictures of prominent players. Price 10 cents.

No. 129—Water Polo.

The contents of this book treat of every detail, the individual work of the players, the practice of the team, how to throw the ball, with illustrations and many valuable hints. Price 10 cents.

No. 199—Equestrian Polo.

Compiled by H. L. Fitzpatrick of the New York Sun. Illustrated with portraits of leading players, and contains most useful information for polo players. Price 10 cents.

Group XI. Miscellaneous Games

No. 271—Spalding's Official Roque Guide.

The official publication of the National Roque Association of America. Contains a description of the courts and their construction, diagrams, illustrations, rules and valuable information. Price 10 cents.

No. 138—Spalding's Official Croquet Guide

Contains directions for playing, diagrams of important strokes, description of grounds, instructions for the beginner, terms used in the game, and the official playing rules. Price 10 cents.

No. 341—How to Bowl.

The contents include: diagrams of effective deliveries; hints to beginners; how to score; official rules; spares; how they are mdae; rules for cocked hat, quintet, cocked hat and feather, battle game, etc. Price 10 cents.

SPALDING ATHLETIC LIBRARY

No. 248—Archery.

A new and up-to-date book on this fascinating pastime. The several varieties of archery; instructions for shooting; how to select implements; how to score; and a great deal of interesting information. Illustrated. Price 10 cents.

No. 194—Racquets, Squash-Racquets and Court Tennis.

How to play each game is thoroughly explained, and all the difficult strokes shown by special photographs taken especially for this book. Contains the official rules for each game. Price 10 cents.

No. 167—Quoits.

Contains a description of the plays used by experts and the official rules. Illustrated. Price 10 cents.

No. 170—Push Ball.

This book contains the official rules and a sketch of the game; illustrated. Price 10 cents.

No. 13—How to Play Hand Ball.

By the world's champion. Michael Egan. Every play is thoroughly explained by text and diagram. Illustrated. Price 10 cents.

No. 14—Curling.

A short history of this famous Scottish pastime, with instructions for play, rules of the game, definitions of terms and diagrams of different shots. Price 10 cents.

No. 207—Bowling on the Green; or, Lawn Bowls.

How to construct a green; how to play the game, and the official rules of the Scottish Bowling Association. Illustrated. Price 10 cents.

No. 189—Children's Games.

These games are intended for use at recesses, and all but the team games have been adapted to large classes. Suitable for children from three to eight years, and include a great variety. Price 10 cents.

No. 188—Lawn Games.

Lawn Hockey, Garden Hockey, Hand Tennis, Tether Tennis; also Volley Ball, Parlor Hockey, Badminton, Basket Goal. Price 10 cents.

Group XII. Athletics

No. 12—Spalding's Official Athletic Almanac.

Compiled by J. E. Sullivan, President of the Amateur Athletic Union. The only annual publication now issued that contains a complete list of amateur best-on-records; intercollegiate. swimming, interscholastic, English, Irish, Scotch, Swedish, Continental, South African, Australasian; numerous photos of individual athletes and leading athletic teams. Price 10 cents.

No. 12A—Spalding's Official Athletic Rules.

The A. A. U. is the governing body of athletes in the United States of America, and all games must be held under its rules, which are exclusively published in this handbook, and a copy should be in the hands of every athlete and every club officer in America. Price 10 cents.

No. 27—College Athletics.

M. C. Murphy, the well-known athletic trainer, now with Pennsylvania, the author of this book, has written it especially for the schoolboy and college man, but it is invaluable for the athlete who wishes to excel in any branch of athletic sport; profusely illustrated. Price 10 cents.

No. 182—All-Around Athletics.

Gives in full the method of scoring the All-Around Championship; how to train for the All-Around Championship. Illustrated. Price 10 cents.

No. 156—Athlete's Guide.

Full instructions for the beginner, telling how to sprint, hurdle, jump and throw weights, general hints on training; valuable advice to beginners and important A. A. U. rules and their explanations, while the pictures comprise many scenes of champions in action. Price 10 cents.

SPALDING ATHLETIC LIBRARY

No. 273—The Olympic Games at Athens.

A complete account of the Olympic Games of 1906, at Athens, the greatest International Athletic Contest ever held. Compiled by J. E. Sullivan, Special United States Commissioner to the Olympic Games. Price 10 cents.

No. 87—Athletic Primer.

Edited by J. E. Sullivan, Secretary-Treasurer of the Amateur Athletic Union. Tells how to organize an athletic club, how to conduct an athletic meeting, and gives rules for the government of athletic meetings; contents also include directions for laying out athletic grounds, and a very instructive article on training. Price 10 cents.

No. 255—How to Run 100 Yards.

By J. W. Morton, the noted British champion. Many of Mr. Morton's methods of training are novel to American athletes, but his success is the best tribute to their worth. Illustrated. Price 10 cents.

No. 174—Distance and Cross-Country Running.

By George Orton, the famous University of Pennsylvania runner. The quarter, half, mile, the longer distances, and cross-country running and steeplechasing, with instructions for training; pictures of leading athletes in action, with comments by the editors Price 10 cents.

No. 259—Weight Throwing.

Probably no other man in the world has had the varied and long experience of James S. Mitchel, the author, in the weight throwing department of athletics. The book gives valuable information not only for the novice, but for the expert as well. Price 10 cents.

No. 246—Athletic Training for Schoolboys.

By Geo. W. Orton. Each event in the Intercollegiate programme is treated of separately. Price 10 cents.

No. 55—Official Sporting Rules.

Contains rules not found in other publications for the government of many sports: rules for wrestling, shuffleboard, snowshoeing, professional racing, pigeon shooting, dog racing, pistol and revolver shooting, British water polo rules, Rugby foot ball rules. Price 10 cents.

No. 252—How to Sprint.

Every athlete who aspires to be a sprinter can study this book to advantage. Price 10 cents.

No. 331—Schoolyard Athletics.

By J. E. Sullivan, Secretary-Treasurer Amateur Athletic Union and member of Board of Education of Greater New York. An invaluable handbook for the teacher and the pupil. Gives a systematic plan for conducting school athletic contests and instructs how to prepare for the various events. Illustrated. Price 10 cents.

No. 317—Marathon Running.

A new and up-to-date book on this popular pastime. Contains pictures of the leading Marathon runners, methods of training, and best times made in various Marathon events. Price 10 cents.

No. 342—Walking; for Health and Competition.

Contains a great deal of useful and interesting information for the pedestrian, giving the best methods of walking for recreation or competition, by leading authorities. A history of the famous Fresh Air Club of New York is also included, with specimen tours, rules for competitive walking, records and numerous illustrations. Price 10 cents.

ATHLETIC AUXILIARIES.

No. 349—Official Intercollegiate A.A.A.A. Handbook.

Contains constitution, by-laws, and laws of athletics; records from 1876 to date. Price 10 cents.

No. 308—Official Handbook New York Interscholastic Athletic Association.

Contains the Association's records, constitution and by-laws and other information. Price 10 cents.

No. 302— Official Y.M.C.A. Handbook.

Contains the official rules governing all sports under the jurisdiction of the Y. M. C. A., official Y. M. C. A. scoring tables, pentathlon rules, pictures of leading Y. M. C. A. athletes. Price 10 cents.

SPALDING ATHLETIC LIBRARY

No. 313—Official Handbook of the Public Schools Athletic League.

Contains complete list of records, constitution and general review of the season in the Public Schools Athletic League of Greater New York. Illustrated. Edited by C. Ward Crampton, M.D. Price 10 cents.

No. 314—"Girls' Athletics." Official Handbook of the Girls' Branch of the Public Schools Athletic League.

The official publication. Contains constitution and by-laws, list of officers, donors, founders, life and annual members, reports and illustrations, schoolroom games. Edited by Miss Elizabeth Burchenal, B.L. Price 10 cents.

No. 347—Official Handbook Public Schools Athletic League of San Francisco.

Comprises annual report; records; trophies; athletic rules; hints on training; constitution and by-laws. Illustrated. Edited by Ray Daugherty. Price 10 cents.

No. 23—Canoeing.

Paddling, sailing, cruising and racing canoes and their uses; with hints on rig and management; the choice of a canoe; sailing canoes, racing regulations; canoeing and camping. Fully illustrated. Price 10 cents.

No. 209—How to Become a Skater.

Contains advice for beginners; how to become a figure skater, showing how to do all the different tricks of the best figure skaters. Pictures of prominent skaters and numerous diagrams. Price 10 cents.

No. 282—Official Roller Skating Guide.

Directions for becoming a fancy and trick roller skater, and rules for roller skating. Pictures of prominent trick skaters in action. Price 10 cents.

No. 178—How to Train for Bicycling.

Gives methods of the best riders when training for long or short distance races; hints on training. Revised and up-to-date in every particular. Price 10 cents.

Group XIII. Athletic Accomplishments

No. 177—How to Swim.

Will interest the expert as well as the novice; the illustrations were made from photographs especially posed, showing the swimmer in clear water; a valuable feature is the series of "land drill" exercises for the beginner. Price 10 cents.

No. 296—Speed Swimming.

By Champion C. M. Daniels of the New York Athletic Club team, holder of numerous American records, and the best swimmer in America qualified to write on the subject. Any boy should be able to increase his speed in the water after reading Champion Daniels' instructions on the subject. Price 10 cents.

No. 128—How to Row.

By E. J. Giannini, of the New York Athletic Club, one of America's most famous amateur oarsmen and champions. Shows how to hold the oars, the finish of the stroke and other valuable information. Price 10 cents.

Group XIV. Manly Sports

No. 140—Wrestling.

Catch-as-catch-can style. Seventy illustrations of the different holds, photographed especially and so described that anybody can with little effort learn every one. Price 10 cents.

No. 18—Fencing.

By Dr. Edward Breck, of Boston, editor of The Swordsman, a prominent amateur fencer. A book that has stood the test of time, and is universally acknowledged to be a standard work. Illustrated. Price 10 cents.

No. 162—Boxing Guide.

Contains over 70 pages of illustrations showing all the latest blows, posed especially for this book under the supervision of a well-known instructor of boxing, who makes a specialty of teaching and knows how to impart his knowledge. Price 10 cents.

No. 165—The Art of Fencing

By Regis and Louis Senac, of New York, famous instructors and leading authorities on the subject. Gives in detail how every move should be made. Price 10 cents.

SPALDING ATHLETIC LIBRARY

No. 236—How to Wrestle.

The most complete and up-to-date book on wrestling ever published. Edited by F. R. Toombs, and devoted principally to special poses and illustrations by George Hackenschmidt, the "Russian Lion." Price 10 cents.

No. 102—Ground Tumbling.

Any boy, by reading this book and following the instructions, can become proficient. Price 10 cents.

No. 289—Tumbling for Amateurs.

Specially compiled for amateurs by Dr. James T. Gwathmey. Every variety of the pastime explained by text and pictures, over 100 different positions being shown. Price 10 cents.

No. 191—How to Punch the Bag.

The best treatise on bag punching that has ever been printed. Every variety of blow used in training is shown and explained, with a chapter on fancy bag punching by a well-known theatrical bag puncher. Price 10 cents.

No. 200—Dumb-Bells.

The best work on dumb-bells that has ever been offered. By Prof. G. Bojus, of New York. Contains 200 photographs. Should be in the hands of every teacher and pupil of physical culture, and is invaluable for home exercise. Price 10 cents.

No. 143—Indian Clubs and Dumb-Bells.

By America's amateur champion club swinger, J. H. Dougherty. It is clearly illustrated, by which any novice can become an expert. Price 10 cents.

No. 262—Medicine Ball Exercises.

A series of plain and practical exercises with the medicine ball, suitable for boys and girls, business and professional men, in and out of gymnasium. Price 10 cents.

No. 29—Pulley Weight Exercises.

By Dr. Henry S. Anderson, instructor in heavy gymnastics Yale gymnasium. In conjunction with a chest machine anyone with this book can become perfectly developed. Price 10 cents.

No. 233—Jiu Jitsu.

Each move thoroughly explained and illustrated with numerous full-page pictures of Messrs. A. Minami and K. Koyama, two of the most famous exponents of the art of Jiu Jitsu, who posed especially for this book. Price 10 cents.

No. 166—How to Swing Indian Clubs.

By Prof. E. B. Warman. By following the directions carefully anyone can become an expeit. Price 10 cents.

No. 326—Professional Wrestling.

A book devoted to the catch-as-catch-can style; illustrated with half-tone pictures showing the different holds used by Frank Gotch, champion catch-as-catch-can wrestler of the world. Pcsed by Dr. Roller and Charles Postl. By Ed. W. Smith, Sporting Editor of the Chicago American. Price 10 cents.

Group XV. Gymnastics

No. 104—The Grading of Gymnastic Exercises.

By G. M. Martin. A book that should be in the hands of every physical director of the Y. M. C. A., school, club, college, etc. Price 10 cents.

No. 214—Graded Calisthenics and Dumb-Bell Drills.

For years it has been the custom in most gymnasiums of memorizing a set drill, which was never varied. Consequently the beginner was given the same kind and amount as the older member. With a view to giving uniformity the present treatise is attempted. Price 10 cents.

SPALDING ATHLETIC LIBRARY

No. 254—Barnjum Bar Bell Drill.

Edited by Dr. R. Tait McKenzie, Director Physical Training, University of Pennsylvania. Profusely illustrated. Price 10 cents.

No. 158—Indoor and Outdoor Gymnastic Games.

A book that will prove valuable to indoor and outdoor gymnasiums, schools, outings and gatherings where there are a number to be amused. Price 10 cents.

No. 124—How to Become a Gymnast.

By Robert Stoll, of the New York A. C., the American champion on the flying rings from 1885 to 1892. Any boy can easily become proficient with a little practice. Price 10 cents.

No. 287—Fancy Dumb Bell and Marching Drills.

A'l concede that games and recreative exercises during the adolescent period are)referable to set drills and monotonous movements. These drills, while designed primarily for boys, can be used successfully with girls and men and women. Profusely illustrated. Price 10 cents.

No. 327—Pyramid Building Without Apparatus.

By W. J. Cromie, Instructor of Gymnastics, University of Pennsylvania. With illustrations showing many different combinations. This book should be in the hands of all gymnasium instructors. Price 10 Cents.

No. 328—Exercises on the Parallel Bars.

By W. J. Cromie. Every gymnast should procure a copy of this book. Illustrated with cuts showing many novel exercises. Price 10 cents.

Yo. 329—Pyramid Building with Chairs, Wands and Ladders.

By W. J. Cromie. Illustrated with half-tone photographs showing many interesting combinations. Price 10 cents.

GYMNASTIC AUXILIARY.

No. 345—Official Handbook Inter-Collegiate Association Amateur Gymnasts of America.

Edited by P. R. Carpenter, Physical Instructor Amherst College. Contains pictures of leading teams and individual champions, official rules governing contests, records. Price 10 cents.

Group XVI. Physical Culture

No. 161—Ten Minutes' Exercise for Busy Men.

By Dr. Luther Halsey Gulick, Director of Physical Training in the New York Public Schools. A concise and complete course of physical education. Price 10 cents.

No. 208—Physical Education and Hygiene.

This is the fifth of the Physical Training series, by Prof. E. B. Warman (see Nos. 142, 149, 166, 185, 213, 261, 290.) Price 10 cents.

No. 149—The Care of the Body.

A book that all who value health should read and follow its instructions. By Prof. E. B. Warman, the well-known lecturer and authority on physical culture. Price 10 cents.

No. 142—Physical Training Simplified.

By Prof. E. B. Warman. A complete, thorough and practical book where the whole man is considered—brain and body. Price 10 cents.

No. 261—Tensing Exercises.

By Prof. E. B. Warman. The "Tensing" or "Resisting" system of muscular exercises is the most thorough, the most complete, the most satisfactory, and the most fascinating of systems. Price 10 cents.

No. 346—How to Live 100 Years.

By Prof. E. B. Warman. Helpful and healthful suggestions for attaining a vigorous and happy "old age," with numerous instances of longevity and the methods and habits pursued by those who lived beyond the allotted span of life. Written in Prof. Warman's best style. Price 10 cents.

SPALDING ATHLETIC LIBRARY

No. 185—Health Hints.

By Prof. E. B. Warman. Health influenced by insulation; health influenced by underwear; health influenced by color; exercise. Price 10 cents.

No. 213—285 Health Answers.

By Prof. E. B. Warman. Contents: ventilating a bedroom; ventilating a house; how to obtain pure air; bathing; salt water baths at home; a substitute for ice water; to cure insomnia, etc., etc. Price 10 cents.

No. 233—Muscle Building.

By Dr. L. H. Gulick. A complete treatise on the correct method of acquiring strength. Illustrated. Price 10 cents.

No. 234—School Tactics and Maze Running.

A series of drills for the use of schools. Edited by Dr. Luther Halsey Gulick. Price 10 cents.

No. 325—Twenty Minute Exercises.

By Prof. E. B. Warman, with chapters on "How to Avoid Growing Old," and "Fasting; Its Objects and Benefits." Price 10 cents.

No. 285—Health; by Muscular Gymnastics.

With hints on right living. By W. J. Cromie. If one will practice the exercises and observe the hints therein contained, he will be amply repaid for so doing. Price 10 cents.

No. 288—Indigestion Treated by Gymnastics

By W. J. Cromie. If the hints therein contained are observed and the exercises faithfully performed great relief will be experienced. Price 10 cents.

No. 290—Get Well; Keep Well.

By Prof. E. B. Warman, author of a number of books in the Spalding Athletic Library on physical training. Price 10 cents.

No. 330—Physical Training for the School and Class Room.

Edited by G. R. Borden, Physical Director of the Y. M. C. A., Easton, Pa. A book that is for practical work in the school room. Illustrated. Price 10 cents.

J. H. DOUGHERTY.
Amateur Champion Club Swinger of America.

SPALDING'S ATHLETIC LIBRARY

INDIAN CLUBS and DUMB BELLS

BY
J. H. DOUGHERTY
(Amateur Champion Club-Swinger of America)

PUBLISHED BY THE
AMERICAN SPORTS PUBLISHING COMPANY
21 WARREN STREET, NEW YORK

INTRODUCTION.

Physical culture is a subject on which volumes yet remain to be written before its necessities are fully grasped or generally understood.

Professors of the art have increased and multiplied throughout the country and yet doctors, hospitals and cemeteries are as liberally patronized as in the dark ages.

Certain favored classes have made a practical study of the subject and reaped golden benefits. Students have had its theory and practice drilled into them at college and have come forth into the battle of life with the physique of gladiators. Elaborately fitted gymnasiums have sprung up in every city and developed specimens of manhood which an Olympian champion might envy. This progress is cheering as far as it goes:

But how far does it go?

The classes have undoubtedly mastered the subject, but have the masses been benefited?

Take any one of the thousands of young men who scramble out to business in New York or any other large city every day after bolting a nominal and tasteless breakfast, and ask him about his health and habits. The answer will only vary as regards his freeedom or otherwise from actual disease. Beyond this he knows nothing on the subject. His habits, he will assure you, are quite regular. He rides direct to his business every morning; stands at his desk, or counter or case for ten or twelve mortal hours at a stretch; rides direct home again, bolts his supper, reads the paper and goes to bed.

Is this man living, in the true sense of the word?

No! He is slowly but surely decaying, without ever having bloomed.

He has occasionally thought of joining a gymnasium or athletic club but never found the spare time. He has perhaps taken a cursory glimpse through some learned essay, lecture, or intricate work on physical culture and was momentarily impressed but did not see how it affected him personally.

It is principally for such men this little treatise is compiled. They can grasp its theories during the homeward ride and practically act isfy themselves in a quarter of an hour after rising in the morning or before going to bed at night that the great secret is theirs.

The only artificial outfit needed is a pair of Indian clubs and dumb bells. With these, a spark of healthy manliness and ambitious enthusiasm, a man can accomplish as much in an attic bedroom, or on the roof in mild weather, as will transform him in the course of a year.

But a youth may argue, as one did recently with the writer "The investment would feed me for a week."

Granted; but there is no visible improvement in the body at the end of a week's, or even a years's, liberal board.

The toiler goes out patiently day after day and week after week to drudge—for what—a living.

All the necessaries and luxuries he can stuff himself with from steak to ice cream in a life time won't make him feel what it is to be alive like rational exercise of those parts of his system which have to lie dormant during his business.

God may have created him to earn his bread by the sweat of his brow to the bitter end, but that does not justify him in neglecting the symmetry of the Image he represents.

Better to aim at having "a combination and a form indeed where every god did seem to set his seal to give the world assurance of a man."

In a country like ours, says Professor Blaikie in his admirable work, where the masses are so intelligent, where so much care is taken to secure what is called a good education, the ignorance as to what can be done to the body by a little systematic physical education is simply marvelous.

Few persons seem to be aware that any limb, or any part of it, can be developed from a state of weakness and deficiency to one of fullness, strength and beauty, and that equal attention to all the limbs and to the body as well, will work a like result throughout.

One of the most effective and agreeable means of attaining these objects is

CLUB-SWINGING.

There is a fascination about this exercise that grows on one with his proficiency. The exertion or strain is rarely felt after the primary motions are mastered. As soon as the beginner realizes that the tendency of the club, from its special formation, is to describe a circle, if not prematurely checked in its course, he has crossed the only stumbling block. After that he has only to think of a movement, and, as a practical instructor puts it, "the clubs do the rest."

The present generation is the first which had an opportunity of enjoying the exercise in this country. It will not, however, be the last, as the Indian club, unlike many equally modern innovations, has come to stay. Its title indicates its origin. When the Britishers proceeded to civilize, and incidentally to annex, India, they were surprised to find the natives marvelously expert in swinging clubs in various graceful and fantastic motions.

The English officers were not slow to recognize the superior development of those most addicted to the pastime. One of them alludes to the then novelty as follows: "The wonderful club exercise is one of the most effectual kinds of athletic training. The clubs are of wood from four to twenty pounds, and in length about two feet and one half."

"The exercise is in great repute among the native soldiery, police, and others whose caste renders them liable to emergencies where great strength of muscle is desirable. The evolutions which the clubs are made to perform, in the hands of experts, are exceedingly graceful."

"Besides the great recommendation of simplicity the Indian club practice possesses the essential property of expanding the chest and exercising every muscle of the body concurrently."

The club exercise soon after was introduced into the British army as part of the drill. In due course its popularity spread to this country and its use may now be described as universal. Indeed, the enthusiast was about right who exclaimed, "No home is properly furnished without at least a pair."

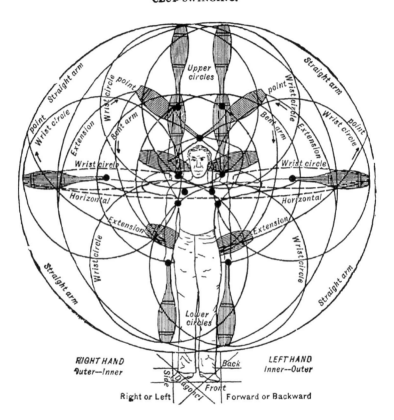

THE PRINCIPLES OF CLUB SWINGING. Fig. 1.

In the engraving the black spots represent the handle of the club and the centre of the circle made by the end of the club in going around The hand being held nearly stationary.

The lines at the feet of the figure, show the manner of varying the movements by swinging in front, behind, at the side and diagonal to the front of the body.

Any circle done in one direction can be reversed and swung in the opposite direction.

Any circle done while the hand is held in any of the nine positions can be done with the hand at any of the other positions.

By understanding this, and the proper method of combining the circles into double movements, the pupil will be able to invent combinations including any two or all the circles.

Accuracy is of the utmost importance in the practice of the exercises described in this book. This should be thoroughly understood as no skill can be acquired when the movements are done in a careless or awkward manner.

It would perhaps be better to first practice the movements without the clubs, turning the arm and wrist n the proper manner until the idea is perfectly clear, then proceed the club.

In selecting clubs the begi ner shoulc be careful not to get them too heavy for the difficult moveme ts; t ub which can be held at arms length and made describe a wri t circle, is best, and the exercise which would be obtained by continuing their use a moment or two longer would be more beneficial than the strain of swinging a heavy one a shorter time.

It is best to learn the names of the different circles and movements as it gives a much clearer understanding of them than could be secured otherwise. In the single movements the es describe the circle itself. In the double, the name indicates movement by showing the relation the arms bear to each other in completing circle.

In practicing, stand erect, expand the hest, square the shoulder and slightly elevate the chin, look straight to the front, lean a little forward so as have the weight centre on the balls of the fee , have the heels two inches apart with the toes spread at an angle of forty five degrees. If there is a line in the floor or carpet, it would be well to stand facing it; make the club follow this line as nearly as possible.

First bring the club to the starting position, with the hand opposite the right breast, the elbow pressed to the side, the knuckles turned out and the club extended vertically.

Start every Circle or Movement from this position. When only one club is used let one arm hang pendant at the side. If a Straight-Arm circle is to be done, elevate the club at arms length to a point directily above, then proceed.

First make the club describe an inner-circle, that is, start it toward the head or centre of the body. Then describe the same circle at the side, that is, at right angles with the line. Then the same digonally with the line, next describe the same circle in the opposite direction or outer, starting away from the h ad or body, and so on through the three circles as before. Then try another circle the same, and as soon as all the single circles have been mastered take both clubs and proceed in the same manner.

If at first the club wrenches the wrist in making the circles, try some other way of holding it, as the whole secret of doing the difficult movements is in ae manner in which the club is held in the hand.

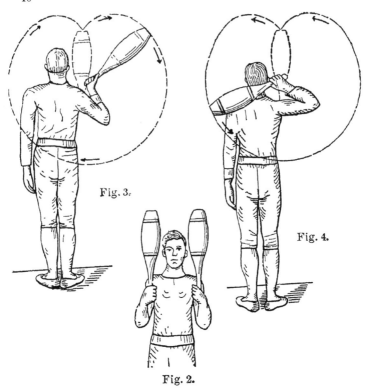

Fig. 3.

Fig. 4.

Fig. 2.

BENT-ARM CIRCLES, BACK. Fɪɢ. 3 and 4.

Hold the club in the starting position, raise the arm and drop the club over the shoulder, make a complete circle behind the back, and repeat. Allow the wrist perfect freedom, do not hold the club too tight as it will make the movement awkward. In the inner circle let the hand pass from the top of the head to the back of the neck.

With the right hand drop the club to the right for the outer circle and to the left for the inner circle, and the reverse with the left hand.

Endeavor to swing the club squarely, and let the evolutions be perpendicular and parallel to the line in the floor.

The only difference between the inner and outer circles is the direction of swinging them.

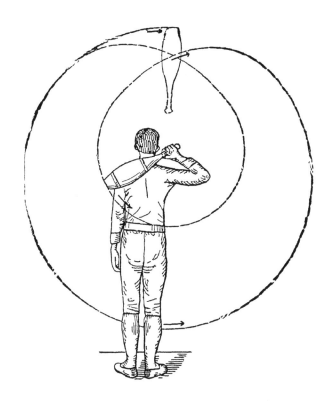

INNER MOVEMENT. Fig. 5.

This movement combines the inner bent-arm circle, back of the shoulder and the plain straight-arm movement or sweep in front of the body, thus making a circle within a circle.

Execute the same with the left hand carrying the club to the right instead of the left.

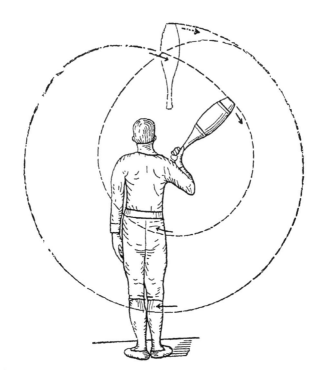

OUTER MOVEMENT. Fig. 6.

This movement combines the outer bent-arm circle back of the shoulder and the straight-arm circle in front of the body.

When finishing the bent-arm circle, raise the arm and extend it straight vertically before starting the straight-arm circle.

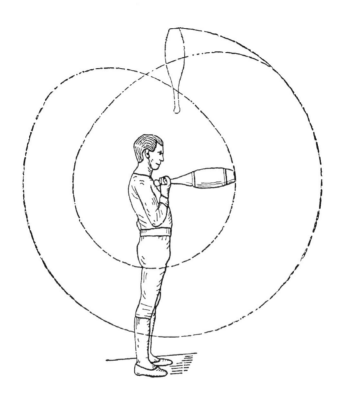

SIDE MOVEMENT. Fig. 7.

From the starting position, drop the club forward or back, letting it turn loosely in the hand, finish the bent-arm circle with a straight-arm, both circles being complete.

The circles should be made at right angles to the floor line.

Repeat with the left hand.

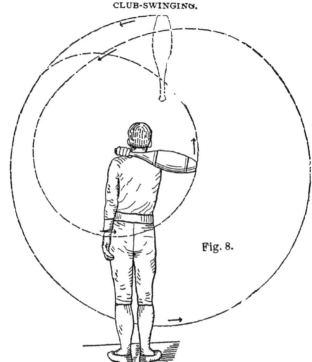

Fig. 8.

OVER-ARM MOVEMENT. Fig. 8.

From the starting position raise the arm and extend it across to the opposite shoulder. Drop the club over it and made it describe a complete circle behind the back. Throw the head back to allow the arm to go over the shoulder as far as possible.

Finish with a straight-arm circle and repeat. Excute the same with the left hand. Reverse to the inner movement.

UNDER-ARM MOVEMENT. Fig. 9.

Extend the arm not in use horizontally. Drop the club with the arm reaching as far as possible, turn the knuckles out and describe the circle behind the back, with the he d c'ose up under the opposite arm.

In the movement combine the straight-arm with the under-arm circle. Reverse to outer-circle. Execut a in the same manner with the left hand.

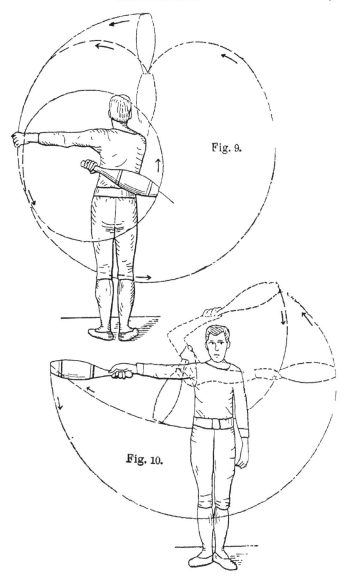

Fig. 9.

Fig. 10.

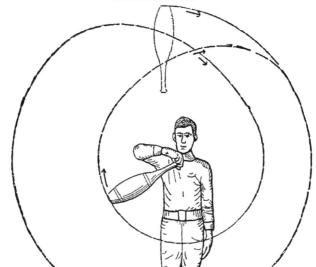

Fig. 11.

BENT-ARM CIRCLE, FRONT. Fig. 11.

Hold the club loosely in the hand, taking hold of the ball of the handle, turn the palm out and drop the club down and around. Keep the hand nearly stationary, allowing the wrist the necessary freedom.

Finish with a straight-arm circle.

Repeat, reverse and execute with the left hand.

EXTENSION MOVEMENT. Fig.10.

Raise the arm and point the club at an angle of forty five degrees upward, drop the club down behind the head and around until it is in a horizontal position, then straighten the arm, from this position drop the club and pass it down in front of the body and up to the changing point.

Reverse the movment, making the club pass in the opposite direction.

Execute in the same manner with the other hand.

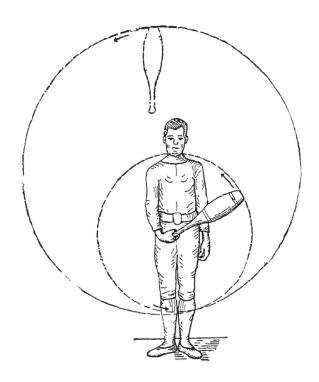

INNER, LOWER WRIST-CIRCLES, IN FRONT. Fig.

From the straight arm circles swing the club around while the arm remains stationary and pendant, using the strength of the wrist and holding the handle firmly. Finish with the straight-arm circle. Execute the same with the left hand.

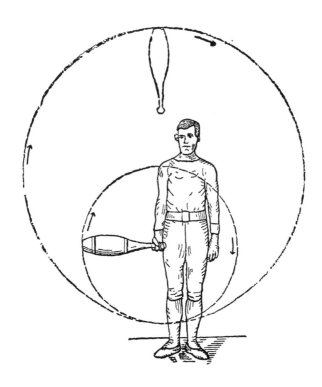

OUTER, LOWER WRIST-CIRCLES, IN FRONT. Fig. 13

From the straight arm circles swing the club around while the arm remains stationary and pendant, using the strength of the wrist and holding the handle firmly. Finish with the straight-arm circle. Execute the same with the left hand.

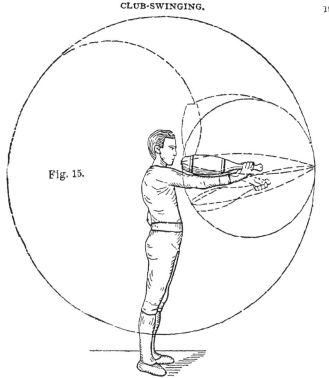

Fig. 15.

EXTENDED-ARM WRIST-CIRCLES, Fig. 14 and 15.

Turn the club in the hand, horizontal, to the right or left above or under the arm, or forward or backward on either side of it.

Let the club roll in the hand and endeavor to keep it perfectly horizontal or vertical. When swung in front finish with a straight-arm circle. Keep the arm stationary.

DIAGONAL CIRCLES. Fig. 17.

Swing the arm diagonal to the floor line, first on one then on the other side of the body, Vary by holding one arm out and swinging the other under it,

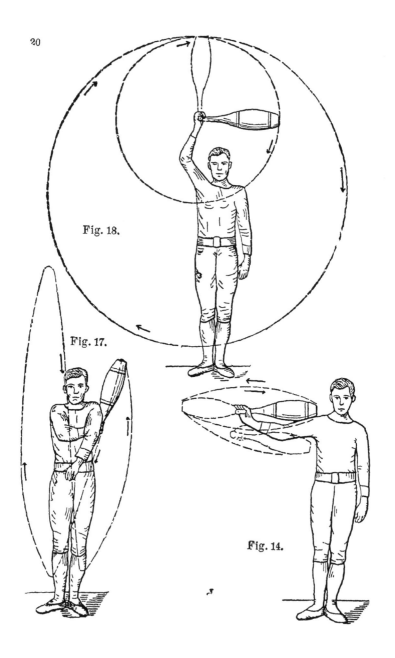

Fig. 18.

Fig. 17.

Fig. 14.

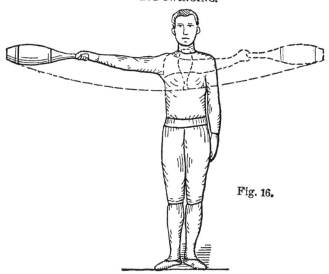

Fig. 16.

HORIZONTAL-CIRCLES Fig. 16.

For the Outer Horizontal circle, hold the club at arms length on a line with the shoulder. Pass the arm to the front, giving the club a half turn outward so that the end of it will be under the chin, complete the circle with the club, passing the arm to the opposite side, then back in the same manner. Understand that the arm makes only a half circle while the club makes one and a half.

For the Inner Horizontal, turn the club in towards the face and across to the opposite side, the arm moving as before. Make a half circle with both arm and club.

This movement can be varied by making the club describe the circle on a line over the head, keep it horizontal as before.

Finish with the lower half of the straight-arm circle.

UPPER, WRIST-CIRCLE. Fig. 18.

After a straight-arm circle, and when the arm is extended vertically let the club drop down and by a jerking movement of the hand make it describe a wrist-circle, then complete the straight-arm circle and repeat.

Swing either to the right or left and repeat with the left hand.

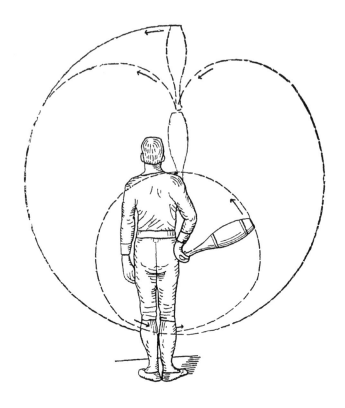

OUTER, LOWER, WRIST-CIRCLE. BACK. Fɪɢ. 19.

Hold the club loosely in the hand or have the handle between the first and second fingers, turn the palm out. Start with a straight-arm circle, give the club sufficient force to carry itself around, allowing the wrist to turn with the club. Stop the arm suddenly, when down straight, make a wrist-circle with the club and finish with a straight-arm circle. Repeat, then execute the same with the left hand

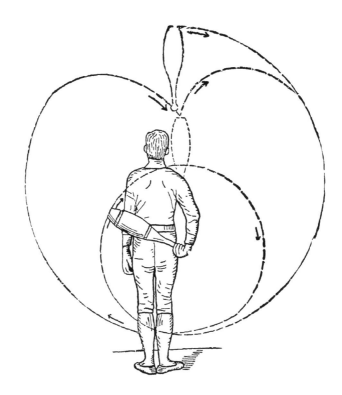

INNER, LOWER, WRIST-CIRCLE, BACK. Fig. 20.

Start with a straight-arm circle, turn the palms to the rear, stop the arm suddenly when down straight, turn the wrist out and allow the club to describe a circle behind the back, the hand following the club to the centre of the back.

Finish with a straight-arm circle.

Repeat and execute the same with the left hand.

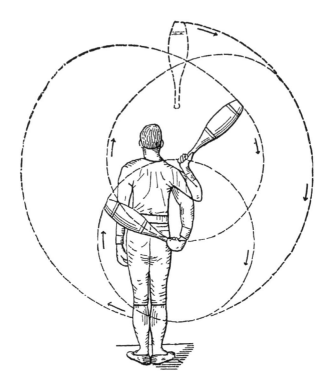

FIG. 21.   Illustrates the manner of combining one or more circles into a distinct movement.

Straighten the arm after each circle.

STOP OR SLAP ON THE ARM. Fɪɢ. 22.

In bringing the arm to a horizontal position, allow the club to pass over and drop smartly on the arm and rebound, reversing the circle. Also by crossing the clubs when extended vertically and slapping them on the opposite arms, then throw them up again, reversing the circle, or extend them out to the sides.

Also by throwing them up and dropping them over the head and finishing with an extension movement.

FRONT BENT-ARM CIRCLE.

Bring the shoulder forward, hold the hand in front of the opposite shoulder, turn the palm out carry the club around for a complete circle and finish with a Straight-Arm circle. This circle is made principally by the action of the hand and wrist. Reverse, swinging with the other hand.

The double movements are simply FOUR different ways of combining the single circles.

The circles described comprise all there is to club swinging. When they are thoroughly mastered with either hand so as to be swung either to the right or left, forward or backward and the same diagonal, they can with ingenuity and patience, be formed into an endless variety of beautiful, intricate and difficult evolutions, by combining the circles.

Any number of circles can be formed into one combination by counting while practicing.

In Single Time, count one for the circle of both hands. That is, in making a straight-arm PARALLEL Fig. 23, or CROSS movement Fig. 24, count 1, add a bent arm circle, count it 2, viz, 1-2, 1-2, etc.

In Double Time, count one for each circle of each hand. That is, in making a straight-arm FOLLOW movement, Fig. 25, count it 1 and 2, add a bent-arm circle, count it 3 and 4, viz. 1-2-3-4, 1-2-3-4, etc. Always count as many numbers as there are circles in the combination.

The REVERSE movement Fig. 26, can be done either in single or double time,

The best method for learning the double movements is as follows. Hold the clubs in the starting position, go through the movement several times with the right hand, then do the same with the left. Repeat making one circle less with each hand, and continue, making one less each time, until the movement is done once with each hand. Then count the circles and proceed, counting as directed.

When the movements and circles have been mastered sufficiently well to allow it, the interest in the exercise will be increased by arranging a routine of movements so as to have them in groups, with all the changes which are in them, in the order in which they should come, with the easy movements first and the most difficult last.

To become an artistic and graceful performer, it is necessary to do every movement in perfect time and with the greatest precision thus combining grace and elegance. If the club is to be held perpendicular let it be exactly so ; if horizontal exactly horizontal Describe all the circles and sweeps squarely to the side or front, and do not swing too fast. Where you can have the benefit of a large mirror, it will be a valuable assistance in exhibiting defects and correcting awkwardness, and it will also assist in developing countless variations and movements. The latter affording an ample field for ingenuity and skill in combination, and with patience and perseverance, the pupil will soon become the master of a beautiful and beneficial accomplishment.

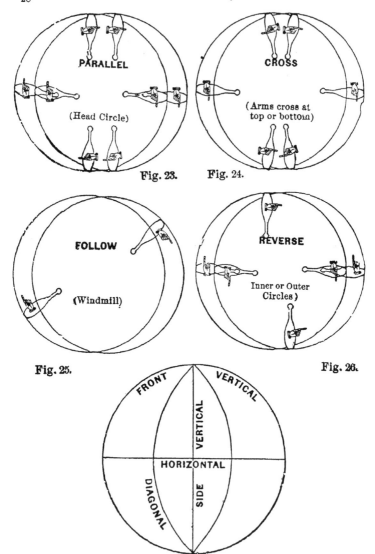

PARALLEL

(Head Circle)

Fig. 23.

CROSS

(Arms cross at top or bottom)

Fig. 24.

FOLLOW

(Windmill)

Fig. 25.

REVERSE

Inner or Outer Circles)

Fig. 26.

FRONT VERTICAL

VERTICAL

HORIZONTAL

DIAGONAL SIDE

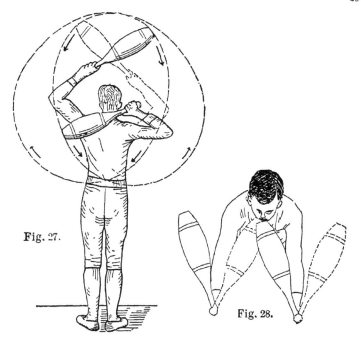

Fig. 27.

Fig. 28.

DOUBLE BENT-ARM MOVEMENT. Fig. 27.

As an illustration of simplicity of the double movements the figure here shown will be a fair example. The movement shown is a combination of the inner and outer bent-arm circles. By crossing the clubs above the head a Cross movement is made. By swinging one in advance of the other a Reverse movement is executed and by passing them both in the same direction a Parallel movement is the result.

EXTENDED-ARM CIRCLES. Fig. 28.

The figure illustrates the manner of doing these cirlces with two clubs. Swing the clubs 1st. Outside of the arms. 2nd. Inside. 3rd. to the Right of both. 4th. to the Left. Either Forward or Backward. They can be done Parallel, Cross, Follow or Reverse, in Front and at the Side.

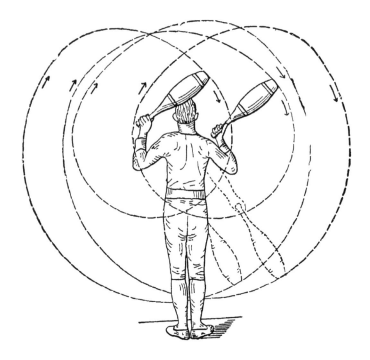

PARALLEL MOVEMENT. Fig. 29.

This movement is a combination of the Inner and Outer circles, the clubs moving parallel for a complete circle.

It is of great importance to throughly understand that the descriptions of double movements are not only for the Straight-arm circles, but also for every circle described in the Single circles. They can all be done in the ways described, and any two or more can be combined.

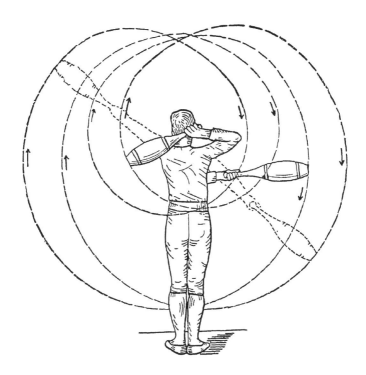

FOLLOW MOVEMENT. Fig. 30.

This movement is the same combination as the Parallel, the clubs following each other like the arms of a windmill, retaining the same relative position for a complete circle.

A back circle either upper or lower must be added to allow the clubs to pass each other.

DOUBLE EXTENSION MOVEMENT. Fig. 31.

The double Extension is a combination of half a Straight and half a Bent Arm circle, and can be done Parallel, Cross, Reverse or Follow, it can also be combined with any of the circles by doing the Extension with one club and the circle with the other, arranging the count, to allow the clubs to pass each other without breaking the time.

These combinations of half circles should receive due attention as it is the only way to reverse from Right to Left or to change from one movement to another without breaking the time.

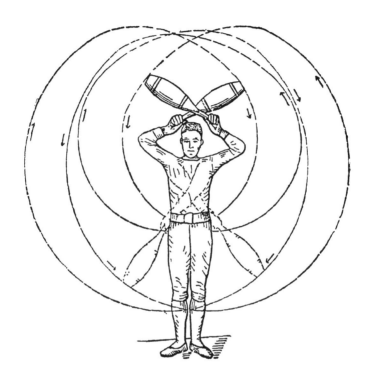

CROSS MOVEMENTS, INNER OR OUTER, FIG. 32.

For the Inner Cross-circles, start by crossing the arms or clubs at the top of the circle and separating them at the bottom, coming together and crossing as before at the top.

For the Outer Cross-circle, start by separating the arms or clubs at the top and crossing them at the bottom.

Combined with the Lower Back or Front circles this movement becomes very pretty.

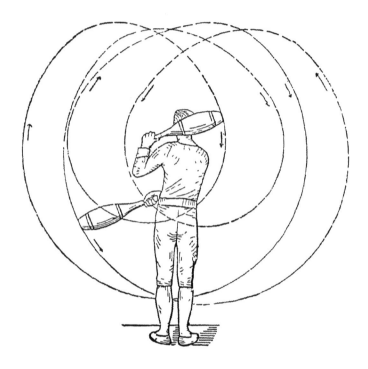

INNER REVERSE MOVEMENT, Fig. 33.

The Inner Reverse movement is the Inner Straight and Bent-Arm circles combined, the arms or clubs crossing and separating at the sides of the circle. Start by swinging one half of a circle with one hand before moving the other, then move both toward each other passing at the outermost part of the circle, repassing at the opposite side.

To combine the Straight and Bent-Arm circles, as in the figure, start both clubs in the opposite directions at the same time, make the right hand club describe a complete Inner Bent-Arm circle, while the left describe an Inner Straight-Arm circle, the clubs regaining the starting position together. Then repeat, making the left hand club describe the Bent-Arm circle and the right the Straight-Arm circle.

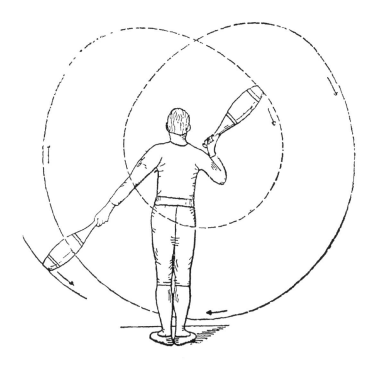

OUTER REVERSE MOVEMENT. FIG. 34.

The Outer Reverse movement is the Outer Straight and Bent-Arm circles combined, the arms or clubs crossing and separating at the sides of the circles. Start by swinging one half of a circle with one hand before moving the other, then move both toward each other passing at the outermost part of the circle, repassing at the opposite side.

To combine the Straight and Bent-Arm circles, as in the figure, start both clubs in opposite directions at the same time, make the right hand club describe a complete Outer Bent-Arm circle, while the left describes an Outer Straight-Arm circle, the clubs regaining the starting position together. Then repeat, making the left hand club describe the Bent-Arm circle and the right the Straight-Arm circle.

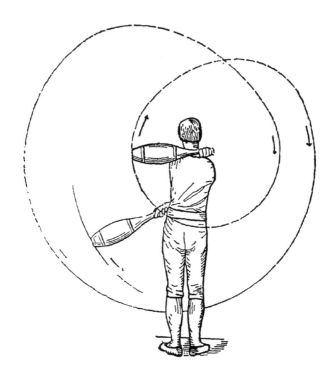

OVER-ARM MOVEMENT. Fig. 35.

This movement is swung the same as the Inner and Outer Reverse movements and the same directions should be followed.

Throw the head well back and extend the arms to their greatest length to allow the clubs to make a graceful circle over the shoulder.

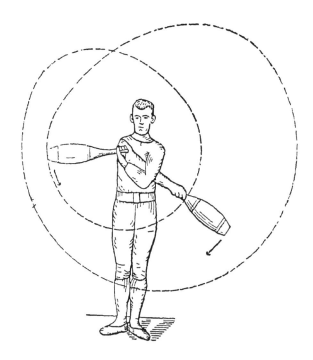

FRONT BENT-ARM MOVEMENT. Fig. 36.

For this movement follow the directions, given for the Inner and Outer reverse circles.

Extend the arms as full length and compress the shoulders forward to allow the necessary action of the arm, making the Bent-Arm circle.

EXERCISE FOR HEAVY CLUB. FIG. 37.

Stand with the feet well braced, as in the figure. From the Starting-Position raise the club and drop it over the head and let it hang behind the back, then reverse the movement passing the club with arms extended, around in front and up to a horizontal position behind the back.

Vary the movement by passing the club to the right or left of the body.

SECOND EXERCISE. Fig. 38.

Raise the club, drop it over the shoulder, extend the arm to full length, pass the club in a full sweep in front of the body and as far up behind as possible, then reverse the movement, carrying the club to the Starting-Position before repeating.

The movement over the head should be made principally with the wrist.

THIRD EXERCISE. Fig. 39.

This exercise is similar to the preceding one and for two clubs.
Raise the clubs from the Starting-Position, drop them behind the
back, bending the arm as much as possible, then return them to the
Starting-Position, make a Bent-Arm circle at the side and in finishing it extend the arms and make a full sweep in front, past the side
and up behind the back to a horizontal position. Then reverse the
movement and return to the Starting-Position.

STRAIGHT-ARM EXERCISE. Fig. 40.

Extend the arm full length, pass the clubs in opposite directions describing full circles. Reverse the movement. Vary the
movements by swinging both clubs in the same direction but having
them at opposite sides of the circle.

Turn the body from side o side to assist the movement of the
arms.

DUMB BELL EXERCISE.

The dumb bell has been used in this country so generally that it has come to be regarded as indispensable to proper development.

Its weight and substance are apparent on a casual inspection but its wonderful influence on all branches of training is only fully understood by the initiated.

Its exercises give fair employment to all parts of the body and to both sides equally.

If the muscles in the left side and arm of the beginner are much weaker than the others, as is almost invariably the case, additional attention to the left hand exercises will soon equalise matters.

In purchasing dumb bells the same precautions should be taken as advised for Indian clubs. Except the beginner is unusually robust he cannot get them too light. They may be replaced by heavier ones as he progresses in expertness and strength.

The modern wooden bells are more generally recommended than metal ones as they are not so chilly to the touch or noisy in contact with each other or on the floor.

The various positions and movements in which the bells may be used are directly and powerfully conducive to erectness of carriage and freedom of limb.

In exercising, keep the head up, and breathe deep and full, allowing the chest to expand to the utmost. The time to take a full breath is when the muscles are relaxed.

The only drawback to the universal popularity and adoption of dumb bells as a means of exercise confronts almost every beginner, not only in the privacy of his room but in the majority of gymnasiums where the instructor is not thoroughly conversant with the rudiments.

The writer can recall numberless instances, where a youth started practicing with dumb bells at home or in some slovenly conducted gymnasium. The method, or, rather, lack of method, was to plug away with rapidly waning energy for a couple of weeks at a few uncouth motions he had either conceived or heard were the proper thing. At this stage the wearisome monotony of the daily grind became unbearable and he dropped the bells permanently in disenchanted disgust.

This difficulty can be easily avoided by beginning properly with the simplest movements. The first few of these thoroughly mastered and committed to memory lead him on by agreeable gradations into the more complicated motions, and his enthusiasm develops in proportion with his muscles.

To lay the foundation for a proper course of exercises effectively undivided attention should first be given to the practice of a series of motions without the bells. They are almost indispensable to a thorough enjoyment of the bell exercises at a later stage and are besides very attractive and beneficial in themselves.

Indeed so permanent is their fascination, that while empty headed and callow youths ignore them as childish, accomplished gymnasts and muscular prodigies such as Prof. George Goldie, New York Athletic Club, and President W. B. Curtis, of the Metropolitan Association, rarely turn out to their daily avocations without going through the whole series with undimmed enthusiasm and belief in their efficacy.

They are here appended in such simplified form that the point may be taken at a glance.

Marginal key words are given in italics to catch the eye and assist the memory.

Place the book open at this page on a rest within range of your eyes, take a mark on the floor or carpet as a guide line and go ahead.

If you have a roommate or convenient companion of similar tastes, you might coach each other in turn from the book and establish a mutual benefit association on which you can draw for life.

FIRST PRACTICE.

Attention.—Position of attention, the toes to the line.

Step to the rear.—Make a full step to the rear with the left foot, the right following.

Step to the front.—Resume the first position.

Step to the rear.—As before.

Left foot forward.—1. Pass hands to the rear across small of back grasping the right arm just above the elbow, with the right hand supporting the left arm under the elbow. 2. Make a half face to the right, by turning on the heels, so that the back of the left heel touches inside of the right, and the left foot is pointed straight to the front. 3. Make a full step to the front with the left foot, the right remaining firm and flat on the ground, the knee braced well back, the hip pressed forward, the head upright, the chest advanced, shoulders flat, the eyes directed to the front.

Recover.—Bring the left foot back to the right.

Right foot forward.—1. Face to the left, the right foot pointed to the front.

2. Step out with the right foot as with the left foot forward.

Recover.—Bring the right foot back to the left.

Step to the front.—1. Make a half face to the right and bring the hands down by the sides to the full extension of the arms.

2. Step to the front, resuming the first position at the line.

Stand at ease.—Draw back the right foot six inches, placing the hollow of it against the left heel, bringing the weight of the body upon the right leg, the left knee a little bent. Bring the hands together in front of the body, striking the palms smartly together and slipping the palm of the right hand over the back of the ¹ chest advanced and eyes directed to the front.

Attention.—Position of attention the toes at the line.

Astride.—Place the left foot ten inches on the left of the line, toes pointed to the front and slightly turned outwards, the right following at the same distance on the right, the knees slightly bent, arms hanging straight by the sides.

Ready.—Bend the knees until they jut over the toes keeping the heels on the ground at the same time. Stoop from the waist and bring both hands to the centre of the line, the hands closed and together, the thumbs together, knuckles to the ground.

Up.—Straighten the back and lower limbs. At the same time bring the hands close up by the sides and carry them to the full extension of the arms above the shoulders. This extension may be repeated six times.

Halt.—Lower the hands to the sides and come to the position of attention behind the line.

Step to the rear.—As before.

Step to the right.—Make a full step to the right front at the angle at which the toes are pointed from the position of attention, the left following.

Step to the left.—1. Make a half face to the left.

2. Make a full step to the left with the left foot, the right remaining fast and firm on the ground the knee braced back and at the instant that the foot meets the ground let the left hand grasp the thigh just above the knee, the thumb inside, the fingers outside, the lower part of the leg and left arm forming a straight and continuous

rine from foot to shoulder, the right arm remaining extended in the line of the right leg.

Face to the right.—Turn on the heels facing to the right reversing the position of both lower and upper limbs.

BELL EXERCISES.

Having become thoroughly familiarised with the foregoing, take your dumb bells, place them on the line and come to attention with your toes touching them.

EXERCISE I.

Step to the rear.—As in first practice.

Left foot forward.—Make a half face to the right and step to the front with the left foot as in first practice, the left hand grasping the thigh just above the knee as the foot comes to the ground, the right arm extended in the line of the right leg.

Right hand.—Seize the bell with the right hand the lower limbs remaining in position.

Up.—Raise the bell above the shoulder bending the arm during the ascent to the full extension of the arm leaning strongly on the left knee and pressing the chest to the front during the ascent of the bell.

In this position the left leg to the knee and the left arm should form one continuous line from foot to shoulder.

Down.—Lower the bell, replace it on the line and recover as in first practice.

Right foot forward.—As in first practice and go through previous motion with bell in left hand and recover.

EXERCISE II.

Left foot forward.—As before.

Both hands.—Seize a bell in each hand, arms passing on either side of the knee.

Up.—Raise the bells above the shoulders, bending the arms during the ascent to their full extension, keeping the left knee bent and pressing the chest to the front during the ascent of the bells.

Down.—Bring the bells straight down by the sides, replace them on the mark and recover.

Right foot forward.—And repeat previous motions.

EXERCISE III.

Left foot forward.—As before.

Recovering right hand.—Seize bell in right hand.

Up.—Recover and at same time elevate the bell above the shoulder to full extension of the arm.

Left foot forward.—Step to the front with the left foot, retaining the bell at the elevation above the shoulder and pressing the chest to the front.

Down.—As before, then advance right foot forward and repeat previous motions.

EXERCISE IV.

Left foot forward.—As before.

Recovering both hands.—Seize the bells as in exercise II.

Up.—Recover and at same time raise both bells above the shoulders to full extension of arms.

Left foot forward.—As before, retaining bells at the elevation.

Down.—As before, and recover.

Right foot forward.—As before, and repeat previous motions.

EXERCISE V.

Step to the front.—As in first practice.

Astride.—As in first practice.

Up and down, ready.—As in first practice, stoop from the waist and seize the bells.

Up and down, up.—The action and position of the ascent as in first practice, carrying the bells above the shoulders.

Down.—Lower the bells, letting them swing to the rear between the legs.

Halt.—Replace the bells on the mark and resume the position of attention.

Step to the rear.—As before.

As you advance in proficiency and strength, either or all of the foregoing exercises may be repeated up to six times. Always begin and end. however, with the performance of those moderate and gentle movements which nearest approach the ordinary motions of your every day life. Abruptness in beginning or ending severe exercise is injurious.

A SIMPLER SERIES.

For any one whose lower limbs are sufficiently exercised in his daily avocations, the following exercises are generally considered adequate. They have not the grace, attractiveness and variety of the preceding ones.

With busy men, however, they are likely to continue more popular, as they occupy less time and attention.

Each motion described is illustrated by a cut, which makes it clear to the veriest novice.

Persons in going through these exercises should remember that by turning the hands they are exercising the muscles of the arm and shoulder differently, and that when the arm is raised its uppermost muscles are doing the work.

It would be also well to glance first, over the preliminary instructions for the other exercises, as to attitude and breathing.

FIG. 1. Hold the bells at the side with the arms pendant. Draw the bells up to the arm pits, turning the wrist as far in as possible. Repeat this and all other movements until fatigued.

FIG. 2. Hold the arms horizontally in front, pass them back on a line with the shoulders as far as possible, crossing the arms in returning.

FIG. 3. Raise the bell from the pendant position to a line with the shoulders, turn the palm out and extend the arm vertically. Reverse the movement, resuming the first position.

FIG. 4. Keep the arms straight and swing the bells over the head and as far back as possible, then reverse the direction and swing the arms down past the sides and up behind the back.

FIG. 5. Hold the arms at the side, swing the bells out and up striking them together over the head. Vary the movement by swinging one bell up and the other down.

FIG. 6. Stand erect, holding the bells at the chest. Step out to the side as far as possible, at the same time extending the arms horizontally. Regain the first position and repeat the movement on the opposite side. Vary the movement by stepping to the front and rear.

FIG. 7. Stand with the legs well spread, extend the arms vertically, bend back as far as possible, then swing the bells down and as far between the legs as possible and up again.

FIG. 8. Bend the legs and keep the back straight, touch the bells to the floor, straighten up and extend the arms high above the head standing on tip toe.

FIG. 9. Stand with the arms extended over the head, bend gradually down, as far as you can, keeping the arms extended, then slowly resume the upright position and bend to the other side in the same manner.

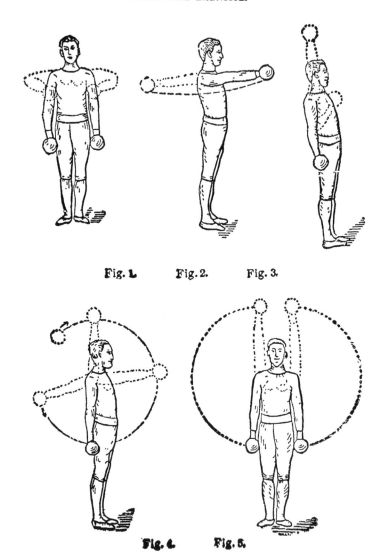

Fig. 1.   Fig. 2.   Fig. 3,

Fig. 4.   Fig. 5.

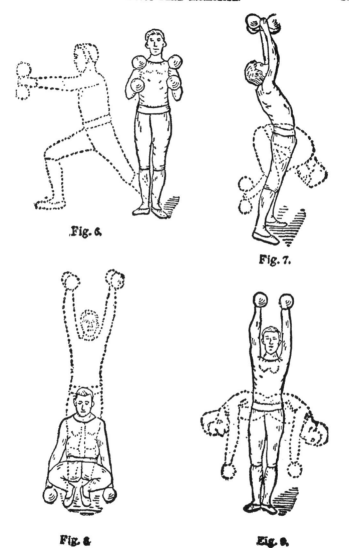

Fig. 6.

Fig. 7.

Fig. 8.

Fig. 9.

SPECIAL EXERCISES.

To improve the biceps.—Stand erect with arms well into sides and feet planted firmly about nine inches apart.

Curl dumb bells until finger nails come in contact with front of shoulder. Bring the finger nails towards you turning the hands inward as you raise the bell above elbow. You can vary this motion in several ways which will suggest themselves after a few experiments.

Muscles back of arm and shoulders.—Stand with body erect, step forward with each foot in turn and pass the bells as far as you can stretch behind you with backs of hands upward. You can vary this motion also. Another method is to stretch face downwards on a mat or form and pass the bells backward in same manner.

Forearms.—Press elbows to side and bring up lower arms at right angles to body. Then curl the hands with and without the bells without bringing the elbow or any muscle above it into play. Continue until you feel the muscles sufficiently tested.

Chest development.—The method most generally advocated for improving the chest muscles is to stretch on your back on a rug or form. 1. Pick up bells and push them up vertically at right angles with the body, the bells touching. Then open the arms quietly and gradually drop the hands until back of them touches the floor on each side.

2. Lower the arms from their vertical position until the ends of the bells touch the floor as far directly behind your head as you can reach.

Then bring the hands back slowly to their vertical position over the chest. This exercise may be varied by letting the hands drop forward until the ends of the bells touch the floor on each side close to the hips.

The hands may alternate in this movement in various ways.

3. Extend arms at full length behind head with backs of hands resting on floor. Then lift sufficiently to clear the arms and describe a downward semi-circle with each until the bells touch the hips. Repeat in moderation.

4. Starting from previous position, describe a complete circle with each hand, reversing the course of the bells at intervals.

5. Let one arm touch the floor, fully extended at right angles with body ; then extend the other arm across the body in same direction as far as possible, without turning off back. Alternate the arms frequently.

I

Amateur Champions.

The Amateur Athletic Union annually holds a gymnastic championship tournament in which club-swinging forms one of the most interesting features. The rules which apply to this event are:

1. The competition shall be conducted by a jury composed of three judges, whose decisions shall be final and without appeal.

2. The judges must place themselves upon both sides of the contestants, in order to observe their general form.

3. The contestants shall draw lots and then perform in rotation.

4. Each competitor shall perform three exercises of his own selection or combination.

5. Except in case of accident to the apparatus, no second trials shall be allowed.

6. The judges shall mark, each for himself, in a ratio to five points for a perfect performance, taking into consideration: 1. The difficulty of the exercise. 2. The beauty of the combination and its execution. 3. The general form of the contestant.

7. The winner of the competition shall be the one having obtained the highest aggregate number of points, next highest second, and so on.

Clubs weighing three pounds each shall be used, and each contestant be allowed five minutes for a performance.

Useful Hints.

If during your first week your muscles feel sore, use arnica; and if a joint be particularly sensitive, it may be wrapped in a cloth saturated with arnica and surrounded by a thick flannel wrapper which should be allowed to remain during the night. This will very soon relieve any soreness which the unwonted exercise may produce.

Cleansing the skin by a copious bath of one kind or another every day is an absolute necessity to perfect and vigorous health. Water is accessible to everybody and is about the only luxury that cannot be used to excess.

One who has not access to a bath room can at least use a sponge liberally morning and night.

A very feasible method of securing a substitute for a bath is suggested by a Boston professor of physical culture. His plan is:

Procure a bathing mat, or make one by sewing a rope into a piece of rubber cloth four or five feet in diameter. On springing out of bed spread this mat on the floor close to your wash basin, which should contain three or four quarts of water. Standing in the center of the mat with bathing mittens on (these are simply little bags made of an old towel), dip into the bowl and apply the water rapidly to every part of the body. The bathing mittens will carry from the wash bowl to your body considerable water. Apply it liberally to the chest, back and arms, and to every part of the body as rapidly as your hands can move. Then, first with a soft towel, and then with a rough one, wipe the body quickly, and with that vigor and earnestness which men display in wrestling or boxing. The feet should receive hard friction, and for a moment, standing with the soles upon a seam in the carpet, twist them from side to side while they sustain the weight of the body. Nothing will warm them so quickly, while the heat will continue for some time.

It should also be borne in mind that daily ablutions, even on the liberal scale pointed out, do not reduce the necessity of a thorough scrubbing in a warm bath once a week

OFFICIAL RULES FOR ALL ATHLETIC SPORTS.

The following list contains the Group and the Number of the book of Spalding's Athletic Library in which the rules wanted are contained. See front pages of book for complete list of Spalding's Athletic Library.

Event.	Group	No.	Event.	Group	No.
All-Round Athletic Championship	12	182	Lawn Bowls	11	207
A. A. U. Athletic Rules	12	12A	Lawn Games	11	188
A. A. U. Boxing Rules	12	12A	Lawn Tennis	4	4
A. A. U. Gymnastic Rules.	12	12A	Obstacle Races	12	55
A. A. U. Water Polo Rules.	12	12A	Olympic Game Events—Marathon Race, Stone Throwing with Impetus, Spear Throwing, HellenicMethod of Throwing Discus, Discus,GreekStyle for Youths	12	55
A. A. U. Wrestling Rules.	12	12A			
Archery	11	248			
Badminton	11	188			
Base Ball	1	1			
Indoor	9	9	Pigeon Flying	12	55
Basket Ball, Official	7	7	Pin Ball	12	55
Collegiate	7	353	Playground Ball	1	340
Women's	7	7A	Polo (Equestrian)	10	199
Water	12	55	Polo, Rugby	12	55
Basket Goal	6	188	Polo, Water (A. A. U.)	12	12A
Bat Ball	12	55	Potato Racing	12	12A
Betting	12	55	Professional Racing, Sheffield Rules	12	55
Bowling	11	341			
Boxing—A. A. U., Marquis of Queensbury, London Prize Ring	14	162	Public Schools Athletic League Athletic Rules	12	313
			Girls' Branch; including Rules for School Games.	12	314
Broadsword (mounted)	12	55	Push Ball	11	170
Caledonian Games	12	55	Push Ball, Water	12	55
Canoeing	13	23	Quoits	11	167
Children's Games	11	189	Racquets	11	194
Court Tennis	11	194	Revolver Shooting	12	55
Cricket	3	3	Ring Hockey	6	180
Croquet	11	138	Roller Polo	10	10
Curling	11	14	Roller Skating Rink	10	10
Dog Racing	12	55	Roque	11	271
Fencing	14	165	Rowing	13	128
Foot Ball	2	2	Sack Racing	12	55
A Digest of the Rules	2	344	Shuffleboard	12	55
Association (Soccer)	2	2A	Skating	13	209
English Rugby	12	55	Skittles	12	55
Canadian	2	332	Snowshoeing	12	55
Golf	5	5	Squash Racquets	11	194
Golf-Croquet	6	188	Squash Tennis	4	354
Hand Ball	11	13	Swimming	13	177
Hand Polo	10	188	Tether Tennis	11	188
Hand Tennis	11	194	Three-Legged Race	12	55
Hitch and Kick	12	55	Volley Ball	6	188
Hockey	6	304	Wall Scaling	12	55
Ice	6	6	Walking	12	55
Field	6	154	Water Polo (American)	12	12A
Garden	6	188	Water Polo (English)	12	55
Lawn	6	188	Wicket Polo	10	188
Parlor	6	188	Wrestling	14	236
Ring	12	55	Y. M. C. A. All-Round Test.	12	302
Ontario Hockey Ass'n	6	256	Y. M. C. A. Athletic Rules.	12	302
Indoor Base Ball	9	9	Y. M. C. A. Hand Ball Rules.	12	302
Intercollegiate A. A. A. A.	12	349	Y.M.C.A. Pentathlon Rules.	12	302
I.-C. Gymnastic Ass'n	15	345	Y.M.C.A. Volley Ball Rules.	12	302
Lacrosse	8	201			
U. S. I.-C. Lacrosse League	8	8			

SPALDING GOLD MEDAL WOOD DUMB BELLS

Special Skill is Used in Turning Spalding Dumb Bells. They Feel Right Because They Are So.

Natural Color, Lathe Polished, High Finish

Spalding Gold Medal Dumb Bells are made of selected first grade clear maple, and are perfect in balance. Each bell bears fac-simile of the Spalding Gold Medal. Each pair is wrapped in paper bag. Weights specified are for each bell.

Model A

⅜ lb. Bells.	Pair, **40c.** ★ *$4.20 Doz.*	1 lb. Bells.	Pair, **50c.** ★ *$5.40 Doz.*
¾ lb. Bells.	" **45c.** ★ *4.80* "	1½ lb. Bells.	" **55c.** ★ *6.00* "
	2 lb. Bells.	Pair, **65c.** ★ *$6.90 Doz.*	

Spalding Trade-Mark Wood Dumb Bells
Stained Finish

Spalding Trade-Mark quality. Made of good material and superior in shape and finish to the best wood dumb bells of other makes. Each pair is wrapped in paper bag. Weights specified are for each bell.

Model AW

⅜ lb. Bells.	Pair, **30c.** ★ *$2.88 Doz.*	1 lb. Bells.	Pair, **35c.** ★ *$3.48 Doz.*
¾ lb. Bells.	" **30c.** ★ *3.00* "	1½ lb. Bells.	" **45c.** ★ *4.50* "
	2 lb. Bells.	Pair **55c.** ★ *$5.64 Doz.*	

Spalding Iron Dumb Bells

Made on approved models, nicely balanced and finished in black enamel. Sizes 2 to 40 pounds, **6c.** ★ *5c. lb.*
Over 40 pounds, **8c.** ★ *6½c. lb.*
Bar Bells, any weight, supplied regularly with steel handles, length 3 feet between bells.
Bar Bells, any weight, with steel handles either shorter or longer than regular length as noted above. . . . . Pound, **12c.** ★ *10c. lb.*
Quantity prices will be allowed on 25 lbs. or more of iron dumb bells or bar bells.

Spalding Nickel-Plated Dumb Bells
Nickel-plated and polished.

No. **1N.**	Dumb Bell. 1 lb.,	$ **.30** ★	*$3.00 Doz.*
No. **2N.**	Dumb Bell. 2 lb.,	**.50** ★	*5.16* "
No. **3N.**	Dumb Bell. 3 lb.,	**.70** ★	*7.20* "
No. **4N.**	Dumb Bell. 4 lb.,	**.85** ★	*8.76* "
No. **5N.**	Dumb Bell. 5 lb.,	**1.00** ★	*10.50* "

Spalding Nickel-Plated Dumb Bells
With Felt Cushions. Nickel-plated and polished.

No. **1B.**	Dumb Bell. 1 lb.	$ **.50** ★	*$5.16 Doz.*
No. **2B.**	Dumb Bell. 2 lb.	**.75** ★	*7.50* "
No. **3B.**	Dumb Bell. 3 lb.,	**1.00** ★	*10.20* "
No. **4B.**	Dumb Bell. 4 lb.,	**1.25** ★	*12.60* "
No. **5B.**	Dumb Bell. 5 lb.,	**1.50** ★	*15.00* "

Savage Bar Bell ⊸⊸⊸⊸⊸⊸

Especially designed by Dr. Watson L. Savage. **Model S.** Has large pear shaped ends with a flexible hickory shaft ⅜-inch in diameter, producing a vibratory exercise, similar to that obtained with the French wand. Per dozen, **$6.00** ★ *$5.40 Doz.*

⊸⊸⊸⊸⊸⊸⊸⊸⊸⊸⊸⊸⊸⊸⊸⊸ **Spalding Ash Bar Bells**

No. **2.** Selected material, highly polished, 5 feet long. Dozen, **$5.00** ★ *$4.50 Doz.*

Spalding School Wand	**Spalding Calisthenic Wand**
No. **3.** 3⅓ feet long. Straight grain maple, black finish. Doz., **$1.30** ★ *$1.20 Doz.*	No. **4.** 4½ feet long. 1 inch diameter. Black finish. Doz., **$1.60** ★ *$1.44 Doz.*

The prices printed in italics opposite items marked with ★ will be quoted only on orders for one dozen pairs or more on sizes up to one pound and on one-half dozen pairs or more on sizes over one pound in weight. On Wands and Bar Bells quantity prices will be allowed on one half dozen or more.

Spalding Gold Medal Indian Clubs

Model, material and finish as perfect as the most complete and up-to-date factory can make them

Natural Color, Lathe Polished, High Finish.

Spalding Gold Medal Indian Clubs are made of selected first grade clear maple, in two popular models and are perfect in balance. Each club bears fac-simile of the Spalding Gold Medal. Each pair is wrapped in paper bag.

Model E—*Weights specified are for each club.*

½	lb.	Model E.	.	Per pair, $	.60	★ $6.36 Doz.
¾	lb.	Model E.		"	.60	★ 6.36 "
1	lb.	Model E.		"	.70	★ 7.56 "
1½	lb.	Model E.		"	.80	★ 8.76 "
2	lb.	Model E.		"	1.00	★ 10.50 "
3	lb.	Model E.	.	"	1.20	★ 12.60 "

Model B—*Weights specified are for each club.*

½	lb.	Model B.	.	Per pair, $	.50	★ $5.10 Doz.
¾	lb.	Model B.	.	"	.50	★ 5.10 "
1	lb.	Model B.		"	.55	★ 5.70 "
1½	lb.	Model B.		"	.60	★ 6.36 "
2	lb.	Model B.		"	.70	★ 7.56 "
3	lb.	Model B.	.	"	1.00	★ 10.20 "

Model E   Model B

Spalding Trade-Mark Indian Clubs

Stained Finish.

The following clubs bear our Trade-Mark, are made of good material, and are far superior in shape and finish to the best clubs of other makes. Furnished in two popular models. Each pair wrapped in paper bag.

Model ES—*Weights specified are for each club.*

½	lb.	Model ES.	.	Per pair, 35c.	★ $3.60 Doz.
¾	lb.	Model ES.			35c.	★ 3.60 "
1	lb.	Model ES.			40c.	★ 4.20 "
1½	lb.	Model ES.			50c.	★ 5.40 "
2	lb.	Model ES.			60c.	★ 6.48 "
3	lb.	Model ES.			70c.	★ 7.56 "

Model BS—*Weights specified are for each club.*

½	lb.	Model BS.	.	Per pair, 30c.	★ $2.88 Doz.
¾	lb.	Model BS.			30c.	★ 3.00 "
1	lb.	Model BS.			35c.	★ 3.48 "
1½	lb.	Model BS.			45c.	★ 4.50 "
2	lb.	Model BS.	.		55c.	★ 5.64 "
3	lb.	Model BS.	.		65c.	★ 6.84 "

Model ES   Model BS

Spalding Exhibition Clubs

Handsomely finished in ebonite and made for exhibition and stage purposes. The clubs are hollow, with a large body, and although extremely light, represent a club weighing three pounds or more.

No. A. Ebonite finish. **$3.50**

No. AA. With German Silver Bands. Pair, **$5.00**

No. A   No. AA

Spalding Indian Club and Dumb Bell Hangers

No. 1

Made of iron and nicely japanned.

No. 1. For Indian Clubs or Dumb Bells. Pair, **16c.** ★ $1.68 Doz.

No. 1M. For Indian Clubs or Dumb Bells, mounted on oak strips. Pair, **25c.** ★ $2.70 Doz.

The prices printed in italics opposite items marked with ★ will be quoted only on orders for one dozen pairs or more on sizes up to one pound, and on one-half dozen pairs or more on sizes over one pound in weight. Quantity prices will NOT be allowed on items NOT marked with ★

Prices in effect July 5, 1911. Subject to change without notice. For Canadian prices see special Canadian Catalogue

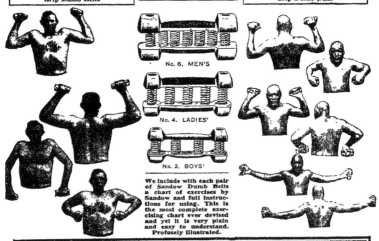

Spalding "Championship" Boxing Gloves

Spalding Boxing Gloves have been used and endorsed by all Champions of the World since the days of John L. Sullivan

JACK JOHNSON

The Spalding "Championship" Boxing Gloves are endorsed by all champions and have been exclusively used for years in championship contests and in training. The material and workmanship are of the highest quality, the fit is perfect, and by their peculiar construction absolutely prevent any chance of injury to the hands or wrists. Each set is carefully inspected before packing and guaranteed in every particular. Made in three sizes in sets of four gloves.

All Spalding Boxing Gloves are Hair Filled. No cotton or carpet flock used.

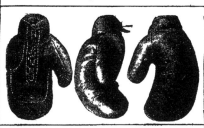

A. G. Spalding & Bros.,
San Francisco, Cal.
Gentlemen·
Please have your representative call at our training quarters at the earliest possible moment, to take measurements for the boxing gloves to be used in my fight with Jeffries, on July 4th. I want your Championship glove, which is the glove I have used in all my fights.
Yours truly,

Jack Johnson

Heavyweight Champion of the World

OWEN MORAN

A. G. Spalding & Bros.,
126 Nassau Street,
New York City.
Gentlemen:
I have used the Spalding Championship Boxing Gloves in all my contests in the United States, also those made by your London House when boxing in Great Britain, and I find that they are superior to anything I have ever used. They are made correctly and have the proper feel, which inspires confidence in boxing.
Yours truly,

Owen Moran

No. 115. The Spalding 5-oz. "Championship" Boxing Glove. Per set of four gloves, $6.00
No. 116. The Spalding 6-oz. "Championship" Boxing Glove. Per set of four gloves, $6.00
No. 118. The Spalding 8-oz. "Championship" Boxing Glove. Per set of four gloves, $7.00

Spalding "Special" Boxing Shoes
HAND MADE. LIGHT WEIGHT

These shoes are made with elkskin soles, which do not wear smooth This style leather is the only kind that is suitable for a first-class boxing shoe sole. The uppers are of real kangaroo leather, pliable and very easy fitting. Being made by hand and of best quality materials throughout, these shoes are very durable, yet at the same time they are the lightest in weight of any.
No. 15. Spalding "Special" Boxing Shoes **Per pair, $5.00**

SPALDING BOXING GLOVES

All Spalding Boxing Gloves are hair filled. No cotton or carpet flock used.

The Spalding 6-oz. "Battling" Glove
None Better at Any Price

No. 106. Made of special quality light tan colored glove leather, very soft and smooth. Plain laced wrist-band, patent palm lacing and patent palm grip. An ideal glove for limited round contests. A popular glove with some of the greatest fighters in the ring during the past twenty years. Per set of four gloves, **$7.00**

No. 106

No. 110

Spalding Pupil's Boxing Glove

No. 110. Made after the suggestion of one of the most prominent athletic officials in this country. A boxing glove that is really an aid to the pupil learning to box. This glove is additionally padded on the forearm and over the wrist, to prevent that soreness which is one of the most discouraging features following a brisk lesson in the art of "blocking." The glove part is well padded with curled-hair, the leather being best quality soft tanned. Per set of four gloves, **$6.50**

Spalding Instructors' Glove, 10-oz.

No. 100. Made of best grade brown glove leather, extra heavily padded over the knuckles and with special large padded thumb to prevent injury to either instructor or pupil. Laces extra far to provide ample ventilation and has patent palm grip. Per set of four gloves, **$6.00**

No. 100

Showing Padding on Wrist and Forearm of No. 110.

Spalding "Navy Special" Championship Glove
Used by the Champions of the Navy

BOXING IN THE NAVY
Copyright, 1906 by G W Fawcett, Washington, D C

No. 18N. Made of a special "sea green" leather, of particularly durable quality. This glove we got up specially to answer the requirements of the United States Navy. Furnished in 8-oz. only, similar in style to No. 118, and with padded wrist and laced wrist band. Per set of four gloves, **$5.50**

No. 18N

Spalding "Club Special" No. 218

No. 218. Full size, 8-oz. Same model as our "Championship" Glove No. 118. Good quality glove leather and careful workmanship. Superior to any of the gloves put out by other manufacturers in imitation of our Championship styles. Per set of four gloves, **$5.00**

No. 218

Each set of Spalding boxing gloves consists of four gloves mated in two pairs. Wear really correct boxing shoes, Spalding No. 15.

Prices in effect July 5, 1911. Subject to change without notice. For Canadian prices see special Canadian Catalogue

SPALDING BOXING GLOVES

All Spalding Boxing Gloves are Hair Filled.   No Cotton or Carpet Flock Used.

STYLES FOR SPORTING AND ATHLETIC CLUBS

No. 11

No. **11**. Corbett pattern, large 7-oz. glove, best quality brown glove leather, padded with best curled hair, patent palm lacing, padded wristband, patent palm grip. Substantially made throughout for hard usage.
Set of four gloves, **$5.00**

No. **9**. Regulation 5-oz. glove, otherwise same as No. 11 Glove. This glove is a better article than what other manufacturers supply for limited round contests. `Set of four gloves, **$5.00**

No. **14**. Regulation 5-oz. glove, dark wine color, padded wristband, patent palm lacing; palm grip. Used by some of the best organizations for their club contests.
Set of four gloves, **$4.00**

No. 9

SPALDING BOXING GLOVES
Styles for Friendly Bouts and Private Use

No. **15**. Corbett pattern, 8-oz., olive tanned leather, well padded with hair, padded wristband, patent palm lacing, patent palm grip.
Set of four gloves, **$4.00**

No. **17**. Corbett pattern, 7-oz., craven tan leather, well padded with hair, patent palm lacing, patent palm grip, padded wristband.
Set of four gloves, **$4.00**

No. **19**. Corbett pattern, 7-oz., tan leather, padded with hair, patent palm grip and patent palm lacing.   Set of four gloves, **$3.50**

SPALDING BOXING GLOVES
Styles for Practice and Amateur Use

No. **21**. Corbett pattern, 8-oz., dark wine color leather. Full size, well padded with hair and patent palm lacing. Set of four gloves. **$3.00**

No. **23**. Corbett pattern, brown tanned leather. Hair padded and patent palm lacing.
Set of four gloves, **$2.50**

No. **24**. Regular pattern, tan leather, hair padded, laced wristband   Set of four gloves, **$2.00**

SPALDING YOUTHS' BOXING GLOVES

ALL STYLES PADDED WITH HAIR.   NO COTTON OR CARPET FLOCK USED

No. 45

Spalding Youths' Boxing Gloves are made in exactly the same manner and of similar material to the full size gloves of our manufacture and are warranted to give satisfaction.

No **45**. Youths' Championship Glove, Corbett pattern, best quality brown glove leather, extra well finished, double stitched, patent palm lacing, patent palm grip.   .   .   .   Set of four gloves, **$3.50**

No. **40**. Youths' size, Corbett pattern, soft craven tan leather, well padded, patent palm lacing.   .   Set of four gloves, **$2.50**

No. **25**. Youths' size, regular pattern, soft tanned leather, patent palm lacing.   .   .   .   .   .   Set of four gloves, **$1.50**

Each Set of Spalding Boxing Gloves Consists of Four Gloves Mated in Two Pairs.

Prices in effect July 5, 1911. Subject to change without notice. For Canadian prices see special Canadian Catalogue

THE SPALDING STRIKING BAGS

THE BLADDERS USED IN ALL OUR STRIKING BAGS ARE MADE OF PURE PARA RUBBER (NOT COMPOUNDED) AND ARE FULLY GUARANTEED

Our single end bags are made with rope attachment carefully centered, making them the most certain in action of any. Laces on side at top, so that the bladder may be inflated without interfering with rope. Each bag is most carefully inspected and then packed complete in box with bladder, lace and rope.

No. G

No. 19

No. 18

No. **G.** This is a heavy durable Gymnasium Bag, suitable for all around exercise work and the strongest bag made. The cover is of heavy English grain leather, same as used in our best grade foot balls and basket balls and made in the same way It will outlast two or three bags of any other make. With loop top. Each, **$8.00**

No. **19.** Made of highest quality Patna kid, the lightest and strongest of leather. Sewed with linen thread, double stitched and red welted seams. Especially suited for exhibition work, and a very fast bag. . Each, **$8.00**

No. **19S.** Same material as No. 19, but furnished with special light bladder and weighs only 7⅝ ounces complete. The fastest bag made, but very strong and durable. Each, **$8.00**

No. **20.** Made of finest selected calfskin, double stitched, red welted seams and reinforced throughout. Very fast and a durable bag for all around use. . . . . Each, **$7.00**

No. **18.** The "Fitzsimmons Special." Made of finest selected olive Napa tanned leather, extra well made; double stitched, red welted seams and reinforced throughout. For training purposes particularly this bag will be found extremely satisfactory in every respect. Each, **$6.00**

No. **18S.** Same as No. 18, but smaller in size and lighter. Intended for very speedy work. Each, **$6.00**

No. **12.** Olive tanned leather, specially selected; double stitched, red welted seams and reinforced throughout. Excellent for quick work. Each, **$5.00**

No. **10.** Specially tanned brown glove leather; double stitched, red welted seams and reinforced throughout. Very well made. Each, **$4.00**

No. **17.** Made of fine craven tanned leather, well finished; double stitched, red welted seams and reinforced throughout. A good bag. . . . . Each, **$3.50**

No. **16.** Extra fine grain leather, full size and lined throughout; welted seams. . . " **3.00**

No. **15.** Made of olive tanned leather, full size and lined throughout; red welted seams. " **2.00**

No. **14.** Good quality colored sheepskin; lined throughout. . . . . . . " **1.50**

SPALDING STRIKING BAG SWIVELS

No. 4

No. 9

No. **4.** A special swivel, made according to suggestions of experienced bag punchers, with features that overcome disadvantages of ordinary style. Rope can be changed instantly without interfering with any other part of swivel. . . . . Each, **$1.50**

No. **9.** With removable socket for quickly suspending or removing bag without readjusting. . . . . . Each, **50c.**

No. **6.** Japanned iron stem for use with platform or disk. . . . . . Each, **35c.**

No. **12.** Ball and socket action. Fastens permanently to disk; nickel-plated. " **25c.**

Prices in effect July 5, 1911. Subject to change without notice. For Canadian prices see special Canadian Catalogue

The Spalding Double End Bags

No. **7**. Made of finest selected olive Napa tanned leather, workmanship of same quality as in our "Fitzsimmons" Special Bag No. 18. Double stitched, red welted seams An extremely durable and lively bag Ea. **$6.00**

No. **6.** Fine olive tanned leather cover, double stitched, red welted seams Extra well made throughout. Each, **$5.50**

No. **5.** Regulation size, specially tanned brown glove leather cover, red welted seams, double stitched and substantially made throughout. . . . . Each, **$5.00**

No. **4½.** Regulation size, fine craven tanned leather and red welted seams. Well finished throughout. . . Each, **$4.00**

No **4**. Regulation size, fine grain leather cover, well made throughout, double stitched. Each, **$3.50**

No. **3.** Regulation size, substantial brown leather cover, reinforced and double stitched seams. . Each, **$3.00**

No **2½.** Regulation size, good quality dark olive tanned leather, lined throughout, red welted seams. . Each, **$2.50**

No **2.** Medium size, good colored sheepskin, lined throughout. . . . . Each, **$1.50**

All double-end striking bags are supplied complete with guaranteed pure gum bladder, rubber cord for floor, lace for bag and rope for ceiling attachment.

SPALDING BLADDERS

The Bladders used in all our Striking Bags are made of pure Para rubber (not compounded) and are fully guaranteed Note special explanation of guarantee on tag attached to each bladder

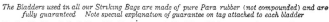

Style for Double End bags and for No. C

No **B**. For Nos. 2, 2½, 3, 14 and 15 Each, **75c**

No. **5.** For Nos. 4, 4½, 5, 6, 10, 12, 16 and 17 Each, **90c**

No. **7.** For Nos 7 18, 18S, 19, 19S and 20 Each, **$1.00**

No. **G.** For No G bag Each, **2.00**

No **OS.** With top stem, heavy bladder special quality. . . Each, **$1.25**

No **D.** Elastic floor attachment for all double end bags, best quality cord. Each, **30c.**

No **E**. Elastic cord for double end bags. Each, **20c.**

Spalding Brass Inflaters

No. **2.** Club size, cylinder 10⅛ inches. Each, **50c**

No. **3.** Pocket size, cylinder 5⅛ inches **25c.**

Spalding Striking Bag Mitts

Will protect the hands and recommended for use with all Striking Bags.

No **1.** Made of olive Napa leather and extra well padded, ventilated palm and special elastic wrist in glove. . . .Pair **$2.50**

No **2** Made of soft tanned leather, properly shaped and padded, substantially put together. . . Pair, **$1.50**

No. **3.** Made of soft tanned leather, padded and well made, also made in ladies' size . . . Pair, **75c.**

No. **4.** Knuckle mitt, well padded. . " **50c.**

No. **5.** Knuckle mitt, well padded. . " **25c.**

No. 1 No 4 No 5

The Spalding Disk Platform

Bag is NOT Included with this Platform

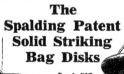

Spalding Home Gymnasium

SHOULD BE IN EVERY HOME WHERE THERE ARE GROWING BOYS AND GIRLS. THE SIMPLEST AND BEST FORM OF EXERCISE FOR THEM.

Combining Swinging Rings, Trapeze, Stirrups and Swing.

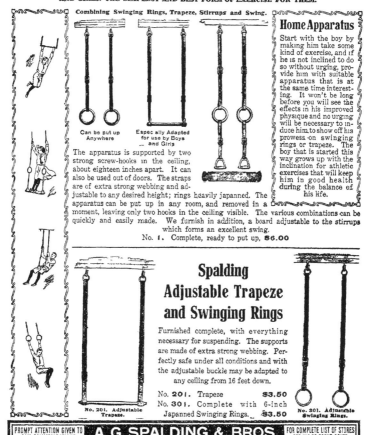

Can be put up Anywhere

Espec ally Adapted for use by Boys and Girls

Home Apparatus

Start with the boy by making him take some kind of exercise, and if he is not inclined to do so without urging, provide him with suitable apparatus that is at the same time interesting. It won't be long before you will see the effects in his improved physique and no urging will be necessary to induce him to show off his prowess on swinging rings or trapeze. The boy that is started this way grows up with the inclination for athletic exercises that will keep him in good health during the balance of his life.

The apparatus is supported by two strong screw-hooks in the ceiling, about eighteen inches apart. It can also be used out of doors. The straps are of extra strong webbing and adjustable to any desired height; rings heavily japanned. The apparatus can be put up in any room, and removed in a moment, leaving only two hooks in the ceiling visible. The various combinations can be quickly and easily made. We furnish in addition, a board adjustable to the stirrups which forms an excellent swing.

No. **1**. Complete, ready to put up, **$6.00**

Spalding Adjustable Trapeze and Swinging Rings

Furnished complete, with everything necessary for suspending. The supports are made of extra strong webbing. Perfectly safe under all conditions and with the adjustable buckle may be adapted to any ceiling from 16 feet down.

No. **201**. Trapeze   **$3.50**
No. **301**. Complete with 6-inch Japanned Swinging Rings.   **$3.50**

No. 201. Adjustable Trapeze.

No. 301. Adjustable Swinging Rings.

SPALDING CHEST WEIGHTS
MAY BE PUT UP BY ANYONE IN A FEW MINUTES

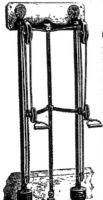

Spalding Chest Weight No. 5

Because of its adjustment feature which permits of all lower as well as direct chest movements, this machine is ideal for home use. The various changes are made by raising or lowering the center arm, requiring but a few seconds. It really combines two machines in one, and is particularly suitable where space is a consideration. Japan finish. Each machine is equipped with sixteen pounds of weights.

No. 5.   **Each, $15.00**

Spalding Foot and Leg Attachment

Illustrating Method of Fastening Foot and Leg Attachment to No. 5 Chest Weight Machine.

No. **2.** Heavy cowhide. Readily attached to one handle or both; can be worn with or without shoe. Each, **$1.50**

Spalding Head and Neck Attachment

Illustrating Method of Fastening Head and Neck Attachment to No. 5 Chest Weight Machine.

No. **3.** Well made of heavy cowhide, Ready for use by simply snapping to one of the handles or both. Each, **$1.50**

Spalding Chest Weight No. 12

This machine, especially designed for home exercise, will be found high grade in every particular. Cast iron parts are all nicely japanned. The wheels are iron, turned true on centers, and have hardened steel cone point bearings. The guide rods are spring steel, copper-plated. The weight carriage has removable felt bushings, noiseless and durable. Each handle is equipped with 10 pounds of weights.

No. **12.** Spalding Chest Weight. Each, **$10.00**

Spalding Chest Weight No. 2

A good machine for home use. Well made and easy running. Rods are ⅜-inch coppered spring steel. Bearings are hardened steel cone points running in soft, gray iron, noiseless and durable Weight carriage packed with felt, good for long wear, but easily removed and replaced when necessary without the use of glue or wedges of any kind. Weight carriage strikes on rubber bumpers. Weights are 5-pound iron dumb-bells, one to each carriage, and may be removed and used as dumb bells. Wall and floor boards are hard wood, nicely finished and stained. All castings heavily japanned. Every part of machine guaranteed free of defect.

No. **2** Spalding Chest Weight. Each, **$5.00**

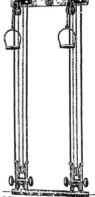

Spalding Chest Weight No.12   Spalding Chest Weight No 2

Spalding Exercising Equipment

Outfit No. H, referred to below, is suggested exclusively for recreation rooms, being suitable for use by those of varying ages, with sufficient equipment shown to supply as many as are likely to be using the room at the same time under ordinary circumstances, while additional equipment may be added as required to take care of a larger number without disarranging the balance of the outfit.

No. H Recreation Room Exercising Outfit

Consisting of	Price
1 No. 12 Chest Weight Machine. .	$10.00
1 No. 3 Head and Neck Attachment	1.50
1 pr. No. 3 Swing. Rings, leather covered.	8.00
1 No. 119 Laflin Rowing Machine.	16.00
1 No. 1 Moline Platform . . .	12.00
1 No. 18 Striking Bag	6.00
1 No. 74 Wall Horizontal and Vault'g Bar.	35.00
1 No. 03 Mattress.	25.00
2 pairs No. 6 Sandow Dumb Bells.	6.00
1 pair No. 5 Sandow Dumb Bells.	2.00
1 set No. 15 Boxing Gloves. .	4.00
1 set No. 118 Boxing Gloves. . .	7.00
1 No. 12 Medicine Ball.	6.00
1 No. 11 Medicine Ball.	5.00
TOTAL,	$143.50

No. H Outfit

Price is F. O. B nearest A. G. Spalding & Bros. Store. *Shipping weight of complete outfit, 570 pounds.*

Outfit No. G is arranged particularly for use in recreation room of a private house. It provides a great variety of simple exercising apparatus at a very moderate cost. The equipment is suitable for use by those of varying ages of both sexes.

No. G Home Exercising Outfit

Consisting of	Price
1 No. 5 Chest Weight Machine.	$15.00
1 No. 3 Head and Neck Attachment.	1.50
1 No. 2 Foot and Leg Attachment.	1.50
1 No. 20H Bar Stall.	8.00
1 No. 205 Bar Stall Bench. . . .	4.00
1 No. A Doorway Horizontal Bar.	4.00
1 No. 1 Home Gymnasium. . . .	6.00
1 No. 600 Kerns' Rowing Machine.	30.00
1 No. PR Striking Bag Disk. . .	5.00
1 No. 10 Striking Bag.	4.00
1 No. 1 Abdominal Masseur. . .	10.00
1 pair No. 6 Sandow Dumb Bells.	3.00
1 pair No. 2 Sandow Dumb Bells.	2.00
1 No. 02 Mattress.	15.00
1 No. 12 Medicine Ball. . . .	6.00
TOTAL,	$115.00

No. G Outfit

Price is F. O. B. nearest A. G. Spalding (Bros. Store. *Shipping weight of complete outfit, 450 pounds.*

PROMPT ATTENTION GIVEN TO ANY COMMUNICATIONS ADDRESSED TO US **A. G. SPALDING & BROS.** STORES IN ALL LARGE CITIES FOR COMPLETE LIST OF STORES SEE INSIDE FRONT COVER OF THIS BOOK

Prices in effect July 5, 1911. Subject to change without notice. For Canadian prices see special Canadian Catalogue

Exercising Equipment of Spalding Home Apparatus

No. K Outfit
Showing suggested arrangement of apparatus included in Outfit K

OUTFIT No. K
Suggested plan showing position of apparatus in an ordinary athletic club room

No. J Athletic Club Exercising Outfit

CONSISTING OF	PRICE
1 No. 5 Chest Weight Machine.	$15.00
1 No. 3 Head and Neck Attachment.	1.50
1 No. 2 Leg and Foot Attachment.	1.50
1 No. 20H Bar Stall.	8.00
1 No. 600 Kerns' Rowing Machine.	30.00
1 pr. No. 3 Swinging Rings, leather cov'd.	8.00
1 No. 74 Wall Horizontal and Vault'g Bar.	35.00
2 No 03 Mattresses.	50.00
1 No. 1 Moline Striking Bag Platform.	12.00
1 No. G Striking Bag.	8.00
1 set No. 15 Boxing Gloves	4.00
1 set No. 118 Boxing Gloves.	7.00
2 pairs No. 6 Sandow Dumb Bells.	6.00
1 pair No. 5 Sandow Dumb Bells.	2.00
1 pair No. 2 Sandow Dumb Bells.	2.00
1 No. 12 Medicine Ball.	6.00
1 No. 11 Medicine Ball.	5.00
TOTAL, $201.00

*Price is F.O.B. nearest A. G. Spalding & Bros. Store
Shipping weight of complete outfit, 725 pounds*

No. K Athletic Club Exercising Outfit

CONSISTING OF	PRICE
2 No 5 Chest Weight Machines.	$30.00
1 No 3 Head and Neck Attachment.	1.50
1 No 2 Foot and Leg Attachment.	1.50
2 No 20H Bar Stalls.	16.00
1 No. 600 Kerns' Rowing Machine.	30.00
1 pair No. 3 Swinging Rings, leather covered.	8.00
5 only No. 3 Swinging Rings, leather covered.	20.00
(For traveling rings — 40 ft. length of room required; 15 to 16 ft. height.)
1 No. 1 Moline Striking Bag Platform.	12.00
1 No. G Striking Bag.	8.00
1 No. 74 Wall Horizontal and Vaulting Bar.	35.00
1 No. 101 Parallel Bar.	35.00
2 No. 03 Mattresses.	50.00
2 pairs No. 6 Sandow Dumb Bells.	6.00
1 pair No. 5 Sandow Dumb Bells.	2.00
1 pair No. 2 Sandow Dumb Bells.	2.00
1 set No. 218 Boxing Gloves.	5.00
1 set No. 118 Boxing Gloves.	7.00
1 No. 12 Medicine Ball.	6.00
1 No. 11 Medicine Ball.	5.00
1 pair 10-lb. Iron Dumb Bells.	1.00
1 only 25-lb. Iron Dumb Bell.	1.25
1 only 50-lb. Iron Dumb Bell.	2.50
TOTAL, $284.75

*Price is F.O.B. nearest A. G. Spalding & Bros. Store
Shipping weight of complete outfit, 1250 pounds*

NOTE.—Where space and funds permit we recommend as a desirable addition to either of the above Outfits, one of our special Wrestling Mats.

No. WX. Size 12x12 ft. Price, $90.00
No. WXX. Size 15x15 ft. " 135.00

Spalding Jacket Sweaters

Sizes: 28 to 44 inches chest measurement.

We allow four inches for stretch in all our sweaters, and sizes are marked accordingly. It is suggested, however, that for very heavy men a size about two inches larger than coat measurement be ordered to insure a comfortable fit.

No. VG. Showing special trimmed edging and cuffs supplied, if desired, on jacket sweaters at no extra charge.

No. VGP

BUTTON FRONT

No. VG. Best quality worsted, heavy weight, pearl buttons. Carried in stock in Gray or White only. See list below of colors supplied on special orders.
Each, **$6.00** ★ *$63.00 Doz.*

No. DJ. Fine worsted, standard weight, pearl buttons, fine knit edging. Carried in stock in Gray or White only. See list below of colors supplied on special orders.
Each, **$5.00** ★ *$54.00 Doz.*

No. VK. Special broad knit, good quality worsted, pearl buttons. Carried in stock in Gray or White only. See list below of colors supplied on special orders.
Each, **$5.00** ★ *$54.00 Doz.*

WITH POCKETS

No. VGP. Best quality worsted, heavy weight, pearl buttons. Carried in stock in Gray or White only. See list below of colors supplied on special orders. With pocket on either side, and a particularly convenient and popular style for golf players.
Each, **$6.50** ★ *$69.00 Doz.*

Shaker Sweater

No. 3J. Standard weight, Shaker knit, pearl buttons. Carried in stock and supplied only in Plain Gray.
Each, **$3.50** ★ *$39.00 Doz.*

No. DJ

No. VK

SPECIAL ORDERS In addition to stock colors mentioned, we also supply any of the sweaters listed on this page (except No. 3J) without extra charge, on special orders only, not carried in stock, in any of the following colors:

BLACK	MAROON	NAVY BLUE	DARK GREEN
CARDINAL	SCARLET	COLUMBIA BLUE	SEAL BROWN

Other colors to order only in any quality, 50c. each extra.

SPECIAL NOTICE—We will furnish any of the solid color sweaters listed on this page with one color body and another color (not striped) collar and cuffs in any of the above colors on special order, at no extra charge. This does not apply to the No. 3J Sweater.

The prices printed in italics opposite items marked with ★ will be quoted only on orders for one-half dozen or more. Quantity prices NOT allowed on items NOT marked with ★.

SPALDING
Gymnasium Apparatus

MANY years' experience is behind Spalding Gymnasium Apparatus. The most thoroughly equipped and largest plant of its kind in the world makes possible the highest grade of apparatus at the lowest cost of manufacture.

Apparatus of the highest grade—Spalding—insures safety to the users, saves the necessity of constant supervision of parts, gives freedom from worry and adds valuable time to the day's programme, does not "eat its head off" in repairs, gives by its durability many years of added service, and proves itself a valuable investment.

Every piece of Spalding apparatus is manufactured and sold under the Spalding Guarantee, and the Spalding Guarantee for 30 years has meant something.

To those contemplating the purchase of Gymnasium Apparatus we solicit a careful comparison of quality. The quality of apparatus selected is a potential factor in the success of the gymnasium.

We will be glad to prepare plans and submit suggestions for college, playground or private equipments. Our experience, knowledge and facilities are freely offered to anyone interested.

A. G. SPALDING & BROS., Inc.

Gymnasium Contract Department   CHICOPEE, MASS.

Spalding's Athletic Library

 FOREIGN EDITIONS

The great success of Spalding's Athletic Library in the United States has led to the establishment of a **British edition,** devoted to the principal athletic sports of Great Britain, and a **Canadian edition,** with matter distinctively Canadian. A number of the most popular books in the American edition will be reprinted from time to time in both of the foreign editions, and, where such has already been the case, the number of the book in the American edition will be found in parentheses.

These books must be ORDERED DIRECT from London or Montreal, as they are not carried in Stock in America.

British Edition
Price 6d. per copy (12 cents), postpaid.
Published by British Sports Publishing Company, Ltd.
2, Hind Court, Fleet Street, London, E. C.

Group I. Cricket
No. 43. Spalding's Cricket Annual, by "McW."
No. 12. How to Play Cricket, by Prince Ranjitsinhji. (No. 277).
No. 17. Cricket, by Tom Hayward.

Group II. Foot Ball
No. 41. Spalding's Association Foot Ball Annual.
No. 14. How to Play Soccer, by Seven Internationals.
No. 47. How to Play Rugby, by "Old International." (No. 335).

Group III. Base Ball
No. 37. Spalding's Official Base Ball Guide.

Group IV. Lawn Tennis
No. 45. Spalding's Lawn Tennis Annual, by H. R. MacDonald, *Evening News.*
No. 11. Spalding's Lawn Tennis Guide, by P. A. Vaile. (No. 279).

Group V. Golf
No. 44. Spalding's Golfers' Annual, by Henry Leach.
No. 10. How to Play Golf, by James Braid. (No. 276).

Group VI. Hockey
No. 25. Hockey—Guide for Men and Women, by H. E. Bourke ("Circle" of the *Sportsman*).

Group VII. Basket Ball
No. 27. How to Play Basket Ball. (No. 193).

Group XII. Athletics
No. 26. Athletic Training For Schoolboys. (No. 246).
No. 8. How to Sprint. (No. 252).
No. 9. How to Run 100 Yards, by J. W. Morton. (No. 255).

Group XIII. Athletic Accomplishments
No. 21. How to Swim and Save Life, by C. M. Daniels, H. Johannson, A. Sinclair.
No. 31. Rowing and Boating, by Capt. Frank Beddington.

Group XIV. Manly Sports
No. 2. How to Wrestle. (No. 236).
No. 5. How to Punch the Bag. (No. 191).
No. 3. Jiu Jitsu. (No. 233).
No. 4. Dumb Bells. (No. 143).
No. 6. Boxing. (No. 162).
No. 26. Indian Club Exercises. (No. 166).

Group XVI. Physical Culture
No. 7. Ten Minutes' Exercise for Busy Men. (No. 161).
No. 1. Muscle Building. (No. 238).

Group XVII. Lacrosse
No. 42. How to Play Lacrosse. (No. 201).

Canadian Edition
Price 10 cents per copy, postpaid.
Published by Canadian Sports Publishing Co., Limited, 443 St. James Street, Montreal, Canada.

Group I. Foot Ball
No. 1. Spalding's Official Canadian Foot Ball Guide.

Group II. Hockey
No. 2. Spalding's Official Canadian Hockey Guide.

Group III. Base Ball
No. 3. Spalding's Official Canadian Base Ball Guide.

Group IV. Lacrosse
No. 4. Spalding's Official Canadian Lacrosse Guide.

Durand-Steel Lockers

Wooden lockers are objectionable, because they attract vermin, absorb odors, can be easily broken into, and are dangerous on account of fire.

Lockers made from wire mesh or expanded metal afford little security, as they can be easily entered with wire cutters. Clothes placed in them become covered with dust, and the lockers themselves present a poor appearance, resembling animal cages.

Durand-Steel Lockers are made of finest grade furniture steel and are finished with gloss black, furnace-baked japan (400°), comparable to that used on hospital ware, which will never flake off nor require refinishing, as do paints and enamels.

Some of the 6,000 Durand-Steel Lockers installed in the Public Gymnasiums of Chicago. 12"x 15"x 42", Double Tier.

Durand-Steel Lockers are usually built with doors perforated full length in panel design with sides and backs solid. This prevents clothes in one locker from coming in contact with wet garments in adjoining lockers, while plenty of ventilation is secured by having the door perforated its entire length, but, if the purchaser prefers. we perforate the backs also.

The cost of Durand-Steel Lockers is no more than that of first-class wooden lockers, and they last as long as the building, are sanitary, secure, and in addition, are fire-proof.

THE FOLLOWING STANDARD SIZES ARE THOSE MOST COMMONLY USED:

DOUBLE TIER	SINGLE TIER
12 x 12 x 36 Inch	12 x 12 x 60 Inch
15 x 15 x 36 Inch	15 x 15 x 60 Inch
12 x 12 x 42 Inch	12 x 12 x 72 Inch
15 x 15 x 42 Inch	15 x 15 x 72 Inch

SPECIAL SIZES MADE TO ORDER.

We are handling lockers as a special contract business, and shipment will in every case be made direct from the factory in Chicago. If you will let us know the number of lockers, size and arrangement, we shall be glad to take up, through correspondence, the matter of prices.

Six Lockers in Double Tier   Three Lockers in Single Tier.

SPALDING'S
New Athletic Goods Catalogue

THE following selection of items from Spalding's latest Catalogue will give an idea of the great variety of ATHLETIC GOODS manufactured by A. G. SPALDING & BROS.   SEND FOR A FREE COPY. (See list of Spalding Stores on inside front cover of this book.)

Prices in effect July 5, 1911. Subject to change without notice. For Canadian prices see special Canadian Catalogue

Standard Policy

A Standard Quality must be inseparably linked to a Standard Policy.

Without a definite and Standard Mercantile Policy, it is impossible for a manufacturer to long maintain a Standard Quality.

To market his goods through the jobber, a manufacturer must provide a profit for the jobber as well as the retail dealer. To meet these conditions of Dual Profits, the manufacturer is obliged to set a proportionately high list price on his goods to the consumer.

To enable the glib salesman, when booking his orders, to figure out attractive profits to both the jobber and retailer, these high list prices are absolutely essential; but their real purpose will have been served when the manufacturer has secured his order from the jobber, and the jobber has secured his order from the retailer.

However, these deceptive high list prices are not fair to the consumer, who does not, and, in reality, is not ever expected to pay these fancy list prices.

When the season opens for the sale of such goods, with their misleading but alluring high list prices, the retailer begins to realize his responsibilities, and grapples with the situation as best he can, by offering "special discounts," which vary with local trade conditions.

Under this system of merchandising, the profits to both the manufacturer and the jobber are assured; but as there is no stability maintained in the prices to the consumer, the keen competition amongst the local dealers invariably leads to a demoralized cutting of prices by which the profits of the retailer are practically eliminated.

This demoralization always reacts on the manufacturer. The jobber insists on lower, and still lower, prices. The manufacturer in his turn, meets this demand for the lowering of prices by the only way open to him, viz.: the cheapening and degrading of the quality of his product.

The foregoing conditions became so intolerable that, 12 years ago, in 1899, A. G. Spalding & Bros. determined to rectify this demoralization in the Athletic Goods Trade, and inaugurated what has since become known as "The Spalding Policy."

The "Spalding Policy" eliminates the jobber entirely, so far as Spalding Goods are concerned, and the retail dealer secures his supply of Spalding Athletic Goods direct from the manufacturer under a restricted retail price arrangement by which the retail dealer is assured a fair, legitimate and certain profit on all Spalding Athletic Goods, and the consumer is assured a Standard Quality and is protected from imposition.

The "Spalding Policy" is decidedly for the interest and protection of the users of Athletic Goods, and acts in two ways:

> FIRST—The user is assured of genuine Official Standard Athletic Goods, and the same fixed prices to everybody
>
> SECOND—As manufacturers, we can proceed with confidence in purchasing at the proper time, the very best raw materials required in the manufacture of our various goods, well ahead of their respective seasons, and this enables us to provide the necessary quantity and absolutely maintain the Spalding Standard of Quality.

All retail dealers handling Spalding Athletic Goods are required to supply consumers at our regular printed catalogue prices—neither more nor less—the same prices that similar goods are sold for in our New York, Chicago and other stores.

All Spalding dealers, as well as users of Spalding Athletic Goods, are treated exactly alike, and no special rebates or discriminations are allowed to anyone.

Positively, nobody; not even officers, managers, salesmen or other employes of A. G. Spalding & Bros., or any of their relatives or personal friends, can buy Spalding Athletic Goods at a discount from the regular catalogue prices.

This, briefly, is the "Spalding Policy," which has already been in successful operation for the past 12 years, and will be indefinitely continued.

In other words, "The Spalding Policy" is a "square deal" for everybody.

A. G. SPALDING & BROS.

By *A. G. Spalding*

PRESIDENT.